THE RISE OF TEA CULTURE IN CHINA

Asia/Pacific/Perspectives
Series Editor: Mark Selden

Crime, Punishment, and Policing in China edited by Børge Bakken
Woman, Man, Bangkok: Love, Sex, and Popular Culture in Thailand by Scot Barmé
Making the Foreign Serve China: Managing Foreigners in the People's Republic by Anne-Marie Brady
Marketing Dictatorship: Propaganda and Thought Work in China by Anne-Marie Brady
Collaborative Nationalism: The Politics of Friendship on China's Mongolian Frontier by Uradyn E. Bulag
The Mongols at China's Edge: History and the Politics of National Unity by Uradyn E. Bulag
Transforming Asian Socialism: China and Vietnam Compared edited by Anita Chan, Benedict J. Tria Kerkvliet, and Jonathan Unger
Bound to Emancipate: Working Women and Urban Citizenship in Early Twentieth-Century China by Angelina Chin
The Search for the Beautiful Woman: A Cultural History of Japanese and Chinese Beauty by Cho Kyo, translated by Kyoko Iriye Selden
China's Great Proletarian Cultural Revolution: Master Narratives and Post-Mao Counternarratives edited by Woei Lien Chong
North China at War: The Social Ecology of Revolution, 1937–1945 edited by Feng Chongyi and David S. G. Goodman
Little Friends: Children's Film and Media Culture in China by Stephanie Hemelryk Donald
Beachheads: War, Peace, and Tourism in Postwar Okinawa by Gerald Figal
Gender in Motion: Divisions of Labor and Cultural Change in Late Imperial and Modern China edited by Bryna Goodman and Wendy Larson
Social and Political Change in Revolutionary China: The Taihang Base Area in the War of Resistance to Japan, 1937–1945 by David S. G. Goodman
Rice Wars in Colonial Vietnam: The Great Famine and the Viet Minh Road to Power by Geoffrey C. Gunn
Islands of Discontent: Okinawan Responses to Japanese and American Power edited by Laura Hein and Mark Selden
Masculinities in Chinese History by Bret Hinsch
Women in Early Imperial China, Second Edition by Bret Hinsch
Chinese Civil Justice, Past and Present by Philip C. C. Huang
Local Democracy and Development: The Kerala People's Campaign for Decentralized Planning by T. M. Thomas Isaac with Richard W. Franke
Hidden Treasures: Lives of First-Generation Korean Women in Japan by Jackie J. Kim with Sonia Ryang
North Korea: Beyond Charismatic Politics by Heonik Kwon and Byung-Ho Chung
Prosperity's Predicament: Identity, Reform, and Resistance in Rural Wartime China by Isabel Brown Crook and Christina Kelley Gilmartin with Yu Xiji, edited by Gail Hershatter and Emily Honig
Postwar Vietnam: Dynamics of a Transforming Society edited by Hy V. Luong
From Silicon Valley to Shenzhen: Global Production and Work in the IT Industry by Boy Lüthje, Stefanie Hürtgen, Peter Pawlicki, and Martina Sproll
Resistant Islands: Okinawa Confronts Japan and the United States by Gavan McCormack and Satoko Oka Norimatsu
The Indonesian Presidency: The Shift from Personal towards Constitutional Rule by Angus McIntyre

Nationalisms of Japan: Managing and Mystifying Identity by Brian J. McVeigh
To the Diamond Mountains: A Hundred-Year Journey through China and Korea by Tessa Morris-Suzuki
From Underground to Independent: Alternative Film Culture in Contemporary China edited by Paul G. Pickowicz and Yingjin Zhang
Wife or Worker? Asian Women and Migration edited by Nicola Piper and Mina Roces
Social Movements in India: Poverty, Power, and Politics edited by Raka Ray and Mary Fainsod Katzenstein
Pan-Asianism: A Documentary History, Volume 1, 1850–1920 edited by Sven Saaler and Christopher W. A. Szpilman
Pan-Asianism: A Documentary History, Volume 2, 1920–Present edited by Sven Saaler and Christopher W. A. Szpilman
Biology and Revolution in Twentieth-Century China by Laurence Schneider
Contentious Kwangju: The May 18th Uprising in Korea's Past and Present edited by Gi-Wook Shin and Kyong Moon Hwang
Thought Reform and China's Dangerous Classes: Reeducation, Resistance, and the People by Aminda M. Smith
When the Earth Roars: Lessons from the History of Earthquakes in Japan by Gregory Smits
Subaltern China: Rural Migrants, Media, and Cultural Practices by Wanning Sun
Japan's New Middle Class, Third Edition by Ezra F. Vogel with a chapter by Suzanne Hall Vogel, foreword by William W. Kelly
The Japanese Family in Transition: From the Professional Housewife Ideal to the Dilemmas of Choice by Suzanne Hall Vogel with Steven Vogel
The United States and China: A History from the Eighteenth Century to the Present by Dong Wang
The Inside Story of China's High-Tech Industry: Making Silicon Valley in Beijing by Yu Zhou

THE RISE OF TEA CULTURE IN CHINA

The Invention of the Individual

Bret Hinsch

ROWMAN & LITTLEFIELD
Lanham • Boulder • New York • London

Published by Rowman & Littlefield
A wholly owned subsidiary of
The Rowman & Littlefield Publishing Group, Inc.
4501 Forbes Boulevard, Suite 200, Lanham, Maryland 20706
www.rowman.com

Unit A, Whitacre Mews, 26-34 Stannary Street, London SE11 4AB, United Kingdom

British Library Cataloguing in Publication Information Available

Library of Congress Cataloging-in-Publication Data
Hinsch, Bret.
The rise of tea culture in China : the invention of the individual / Bret Hinsch.
pages cm
Includes bibliographical references and index.
ISBN 978-1-4422-5178-6 (cloth : alk. paper) — ISBN 978-1-4422-5179-3 (electronic)
1. Tea—Social aspects—China. I. Title.
GT2907.C6H55 2015
394.1'50951—dc23
2015026485

™ The paper used in this publication meets the minimum requirements of American National Standard for Information Sciences Permanence of Paper for Printed Library Materials, ANSI/NISO Z39.48-1992.

Printed in the United States of America

CONTENTS

TIMELINE OF MAJOR CHINESE DYNASTIES

Shang	ca. 1600–1046 BCE
Zhou	1046–256 BCE
Han	206 BCE–220 CE
Jin	265–420
Tang	618–907
Song	960–1279
Northern Song	960–1126
Southern Song	1127–1279
Yuan	1271–1368
Ming	1368–1644
Qing	1644–1911

INTRODUCTION

What is so special about tea? Billions of people around the world enjoy many other beverages, sometimes to the point of fetish. Coffee does far more than just wake us up in the morning. Besides providing jobs for farmers and baristas, it also spawns convivial neighborhood venues where patrons can relax, chat, and play with their phones. The global soft drink industry has somehow managed to convince huge numbers of consumers that a fizzy sweet liquid embodies youth and fun. Other beverages, from craft beer to fruit juice, also have large numbers of enthusiastic drinkers. Nevertheless, however important these other beverages might be in certain respects, no other drink is as important to a culture as Chinese tea.

The place of wine in Western culture presents the closest social and cultural analogue to Chinese tea. The French have even taken wine to symbolize their national identity, using it as a liquescent weapon to fend off incursions of foreign customs.[1] From the Roman author Horace down to Jonathan Swift and Amy Lowell, the god Bacchus has also inspired great literature. Serious researchers in white lab coats study the health benefits of wine, *bon vivants* idolize it, and Robert Parker meticulously quantifies it. But for all that wine signifies in the West, tea has had far more influence on the development of Chinese culture.

This book does not present a general history of Chinese tea. Several studies in Chinese and Japanese provide eloquent overviews of that worthy subject. Instead I focus more specifically on some of the most important meanings and uses tea assumed within the cultural context of imperial China. In particular, I try to unravel a fascinating conundrum: why did the Chinese perceive tea as so richly meaningful when people in most other places consider it little more than a pleasant drink? The triviality of tea in most of the world proves that, however delicious and varied, the dried leaves of this bitter herb lack inherent profundity. Even so, the Chinese somehow managed to imbue this drink with manifold connotations, elevating it into a key cultural practice and national icon.

The case of tea also illustrates a much larger problem of how and why people in imperial China deployed material culture to serve useful ends. Members of the elite embraced tea and other cultured practices to realize numerous benefits, such as raising their social status, building connections, proving exemplary manhood, and accumulating cultural capital. Although this book explores the culture that grew up around tea, similar investigations could be conducted to elucidate the meanings and uses of jade, flower arranging, garden design, or the appreciation of incense or scholar's stones. The ubiquity of tea, however, makes it ideal for understanding how educated Chinese exploited material culture for personal gain.

Because the history of tea in China covers such a long stretch of time, a single book cannot possibly delve very far into the particulars of each era. So instead of trying to explore the culture of tea drinking in every period, I focus on the Tang and Song dynasties (from roughly the seventh to the thirteenth century of the Common Era), the time when the most crucial transitions in views toward tea took place. Prior to the Tang, although some people already consumed this beverage regularly, tea drinking was still mostly a regional custom limited to China's far south. During the Tang and Song, however, tea became the drink of choice across China. As tea became increasingly commonplace, it steadily accrued significance and became integrated into prestigious activities. In short, during the pivotal age of the Tang and Song dynasties, tea went from being a marginal southern drink to become a locus of some of China's most important cultural practices.

Although Tang and Song can be spoken of in tandem when referring to the early rise of tea, in fact these two dynasties differed in many ways, with the transition between the two periods marking fundamental cultural and social shifts. It so happened that the rise of tea culture occurred during one of the most important periods of transformation in the long history of Chinese civilization. Drinkers promoted tea from a simple dried herb infused in hot water into a token of sophistication and prestige largely in response to momentous changes within society as a whole. As China changed, people altered the ways they drank tea in response. Ultimately these sophisticated ideas about tea drinking spread beyond China's borders to influence other cultures as well, most notably Korea and Japan.

Although innovative, the rise of tea culture in China cannot be declared unique or unprecedented. For example, the historian Shen Songqin has compared the emergence of sophisticated tea drinking in China to the burgeoning culture of the Italian Renaissance, a provocative insight that helps illuminate the significance of tea to the development of Chinese civilization. Although these two cultural movements occurred in distant places and involved very different ideas and activities, Shen nevertheless considers them largely similar, both in impact and kind. Most fundamentally, he points out that during both of these two movements, the elites employed standardized activities and language to construct new modes of highly refined culture.[2]

We can take this argument even further, noting that polished gentlemen in both Song China and Quattrocento Italy devoted considerable time and effort to mastering cultured practices. In light of some key commonalities in the mentalities of those two societies, directing time and resources to this end made sense, as flaunting good taste before peers could win a gentleman considerable prestige. Both the Italian humanist and the Song literatus realized that in order to be recognized as a member of the elite, a gentleman could not simply imitate standard patterns of behavior. To be considered superior, he had to somehow become distinct, cultivating himself to bring out unique qualities and achievements for public display.

In other words, insightful gentlemen in these two distant civilizations grasped the profound insight that, to a significant extent, the individual can create himself. The cultured man's identity does not simply emerge naturally (and they usually thought about these issues in terms of men rather than women). Instead, he gradually fashions a cultured persona, steadily refining himself into a polished gentleman worthy of admiration. An ambitious person who takes the initiative can nurture his special qualities to create an exceptional identity, thereby winning respect and status.

Given the utility of tea culture in creating and magnifying social distinctions, this subject offers a fascinating entrée for understanding the development of Chinese ideas concerning individualism. Tea culture facilitated, and sometimes even demanded, a degree of individual expression. This keen awareness of the utility of personal uniqueness runs counter to the blunt Western stereotype that Chinese lack any sense of individualism. To many Americans and Europeans, emphasis on the uniqueness of each individual constitutes a cornerstone of their culture. They often contrast their own individualism with the group-oriented ethos found in many other cultures to claim this as a unique aspect of Western identity. However, denying individualism to China and other peoples presents this matter in overly simplistic terms. Although Chinese valued the family and other groups, they held a very clear consciousness of the distinct individual as well.

Chinese views concerning the individual shifted over the ages, as thinkers of various persuasions alternately celebrated or condemned individual distinction. Of course Chinese ideas about the individual always differed somewhat from those in the West. Most fundamentally, rather than seeing individualism as an inner essence within the person, Chinese emphasized how people distinguish themselves from one another within the inescapable framework of the social matrix. Chinese thinkers always saw individualism as relational rather than absolute. As a result of the social perspective toward individual difference, appreciating how someone expressed individualistic ideas and behaviors via common activities such as tea drinking could highlight his special qualities.

During both the Italian Renaissance and Tang/Song China, the general mentality underwent profound changes, making individualism into an important and useful cultural trait. Significantly, people in both places used cultured activities to create novel personas and inventive modes of self-understanding. While experimenting with their public image, innovative gentlemen embraced novel types of expression, aesthetics, values, and lifestyles. These daring new forms of self-expression pushed culture forward.

This nexus between individualism and cultural effervescence offers an avenue for appreciating both eras of transition. In assessing the Renaissance, the historian Jacob Burckhardt (1818–1897) recognized how a radical new view of the individual propelled this movement to lofty heights. During the late Middle Ages, the decline of European feudalism frayed the link between heredity and status. With social standing increasingly fluid, behaving in a conventional manner no longer brought the greatest public esteem. Instead of just conforming to time-tested templates of behavior, the ambitious man now strove to stand out from the herd by deliberately nurturing distinctions between himself and others.

The Renaissance author Baldassare Castiglione (1478–1529) believed that the ideal gentleman ought to be educated, mannerly, amusing, moral, prudent, graceful, and handsome. He should also boast a range of cultured abilities, such as dancing, drawing, writing, and familiarity with foreign and ancient languages. In other words, Castiglione stressed that the gentleman should stake a claim to social superiority by highlighting his own unique opinions, erudition, manners, adornment, talents, and taste, thus creating a superior persona that draws others to him.

> Therefore, besides his noble birth, I would wish the Courtier favored in this other respect, and endowed by nature not only with talent and with beauty of countenance and person, but with that certain grace which we call an "air," which shall make him at first sight pleasing and lovable to all who see him; and let this be an adornment informing and attending all his actions, giving the promise outwardly that such a one is worthy of the company and favor of every great lord.[3]

Burckhardt explained the sudden surge in attention to individual talent and achievement during the Renaissance. He pointed out that when personal worth could no longer simply be inherited, society began to reward the creative genius who succeeded in setting himself apart from others by proving himself uniquely refined and accomplished.

> But in proportion as distinctions of birth ceased to confer any special privilege was the individual himself compelled to make the most of his personal qualities, and society to find its worth and claim in itself. The demeanor of individuals and all the higher forms of social intercourse became ends pursued with a deliberate and artistic purpose.[4]

In the wake of this startlingly provocative new mentality, creativity flourished. Society no longer suppressed individual traits as divisive or unorthodox. Instead, popular opinion lauded individual distinctions as expressions of creative brilliance.

> To the discovery of the outside world the Renaissance added a still greater achievement by first discerning and bringing to light the full, whole nature of man. This period, as we have seen, first gave the highest development to individuality, and then led the individual to the most zealous and thorough study of himself in all forms and under all conditions. Indeed, the development of personality is essentially involved in the recognition of it in oneself and in others.[5]

Although Burckhardt wrote about Italy in the late Middle Ages, he could just as well have been describing China during the Tang/Song transition. A strikingly similar process played out on the other side of the globe. Like their Italian counterparts, Chinese gentlemen employed tea culture and other civilized pursuits to win approbation for their special individual accomplishments, thus forging a distinctive public image that could bring them praise and honor.

Chinese had not always regarded individual distinctions so highly. For example, neither Confucius (551–479 BCE) nor Mencius (ca. 372–ca. 289 BCE) envisioned the ideal person as unique. To the contrary, they assumed that a completely autonomous person would likely end up coarse and immoral, threatening social order. These influential early thinkers believed that we do not live the good life by highlighting our differences with other people. The good and meaningful life results from socializing oneself into time-tested roles passed down from wise ancestors. Due to their overweening faith in the value of conventional customs and ideas, early Confucians did not view the individual as detached from the social matrix. Instead they sought to comprehend how a person can best integrate into the wider world.

During the Han dynasty (206 BCE–220 CE), elite thinkers continued to regard personal feelings and innovative ideas with deep suspicion. They assured their readers that rejecting traditional standards of conduct to follow personal passions would likely lead toward immorality. Instead of acting on random emotions and whims, they counseled people to look to the rites and canonical virtues for guidance. The vast ritual canon contains myriad rules regulating important social situations, while Confucian ethics supplies more general principles to govern circumstances not covered by specific regulations. Of course conforming to these restrictive norms requires the sustained suppression of individual desires. People of the time took pride in their ability to subdue cravings and heterodox ideas in favor of approved behavior. As a result of this conformist attitude, Han dynasty art and literature rarely reveal authentic ideas and feelings. Instead, creators strove to present an honorable and conformist face to the world. To gain approbation, people adhered to conventional expectations rather than exposing unique idiosyncrasies and passions.

During the Han, Confucian ritual and ethics become closely identified with the political system. Initially, close integration with the state imbued classical scholarship, ritual studies, and Confucian ethics with unprecedented authority and impact. To prepare for a position in government, students studied and internalized these restrictive mores, suppressing any idiosyncrasies and living out their lives according to this restraining code of prescribed behavior. Instead of creative novelty, standardization became a prime goal in scholarship, art, and even daily life.

Since antiquity, Chinese men of talent had always been eager to serve in government, such that public office became a sought-after confirmation of status and achievement. But as the Han state decayed during the second century, some prominent gentlemen ostentatiously withdrew from public life, startling and disconcerting their peers. With the realm descending into chaos, a weighty sense of anomie fostered pervasive disenchantment. The estrangement of intelligent men from a failing society took many forms. Some took refuge in witty conversation, while others turned away from practical affairs to ponder philosophical abstractions. Regardless of which path they took, these cultural dissenters abandoned collective concerns and practical matters to cultivate their individual tastes. In a decayed era, when speaking truth to power could prove fatal, losing oneself in personal pursuits, even to the point of eccentricity, emerged as a canny strategy for survival.

This overweening sense of disappointment ultimately brought unexpectedly positive consequences. As the imperial order frayed, social norms loosened their hold.[6] New ways of thinking about life and the human being emerged, stimulating an unexpected burst of cultural and intellectual dynamism amid society's general decay. Scholars call this movement Jian'an culture, naming it after the reign era (lasting from CE 196 to 220) immediately prior to the fall of the Eastern Han dynasty. This brief burst of cultural effervescence occurred just as China collapsed into a battleground for internecine struggles between warlords, eunuchs, imperial consort kin, and peasant rebels. The resulting devastation ruined countless lives. However, stifling social and intellectual constraints decayed along with the dynasty that had upheld them, opening up new opportunities and freedoms.

Artists and thinkers seemed almost giddy as they pondered the possibilities unleashed by the breakdown of arbitrary restrictions. Instead of writing bombastic tributes to imperial glory, poets employed an intimate style to explore deeply personal concerns. Scholars lost interest in arid classical studies, turning their attention to innovative speculations about metaphysics. And rather than viewing individuals merely as representatives of standardized social types, prominent men discussed the characteristics that set the uniquely talented apart from the crowd.[7]

Averting their eyes from the catastrophes brought about by the collapse of government and social order, scholars and artists increasingly looked inward to probe themselves. The resulting discovery of the individual marked a revolutionary turning point in Chinese culture. A vibrant spirit of creativity and individualism played out over the following centuries as poets, artists, monks, and philosophers investigated unique individual characteristics. Although their discussions sometimes devolved into shallow gossip about trivial quirks and oddities, this new mode of discourse encompassed serious matters as well. Over time, rigorous interrogation of the individual conditioned both elite thinkers and ordinary people alike to accept the idea that human beings cannot be seen as mere representatives of stock social types. They realized that each person possesses a distinctive personality and might be capable of rare achievements. So instead of suppressing difference with suffocating ritual regulations, some influential thinkers encouraged people to nurture their humanity by developing and displaying special traits.

Growing awareness of the uniqueness of each individual exerted a profound impact on the development of Chinese culture. For example, poets began to explore novel themes, such as the poignant musings of a lonely woman abandoned in her empty boudoir. Philosophers emphasized the value of naturalism, teaching that untrammeled behavior can allow us to lead the best possible life. And rather than representing social ideals removed from daily experience, artists portrayed people in informal settings, undertaking ordinary activities.

During the early medieval era following the fall of the Han dynasty, revulsion toward interminable war and anarchy turned men of learning away from collective concerns. Having realized the uniqueness of each individual, they cultivated personal pursuits and discussed exceptional traits in their peers. Literature of the time vividly documents this individualistic turn. Instead of expressing standard social archetypes or celebrating the conventional and powerful, the poet Tao Qian (also known as Tao Yuanming, 365–427) vented his frustration and disappointment with the world. He spurned the predictable career of honorable and lucrative government service, instead posing as a happy drunkard and lauding the naïve pleasures of rural life. The sophisticated Ji Kang (223–262) acted out his disillusionment by affecting a scandalous disregard for decorum. Uninterested in upholding hollow social conventions, he turned his back on pretentious company and sought consolation in music. As for Ruan Ji (210–263), observers of the time regarded his behavior as simply weird. Sometimes he took long walks in the hills, only to come home bitterly weeping. He could shut himself away for months at a time and do nothing but read all day. He also exhibited a talent for whistling. Not surprisingly, many people considered him a madman. Even so, insightful readers treated him with guarded respect, realizing that this odd behavior represented a project of intense and inventive self-exploration.

Although the discovery of the individual may have been initially driven by frustration and disappointment, this energizing viewpoint gave rise to a celebration of distinctive genius. Ambitious gentlemen realized that in order to excel, they had to differentiate themselves from the crowd. Simply fitting smoothly into the social order might bring contentment and conventional success, and even help steady society, but it could not presage greatness. To rise above mediocrity, the creative individual must cultivate distinctive traits.

The importance of individual excellence surged as hereditary privilege declined. The Kyoto school of historiography guided by Naitō Konan has argued that the transition from the Tang to the Song dynasty, contiguous yet quite different in many ways, marks the most important transition in imperial Chinese history.[8] Among these fundamental changes, elite status developed new footings. During the Tang, the elite generally inherited their status, with most people's position in society fixed from birth. However, the unusually violent chaos in the closing decades of the Tang virtually wiped out the leading aristocratic families.[9] After the disappearance of the former elite, a new and very different social system subsequently emerged. The flourishing commercial economy and meritocratic bureaucracy of the Song allowed people to change station far more readily. Able men enjoyed new opportunities and sometimes rose considerably in status.

Social fluidity also brought immense pressures. Concurrent with the potential to transcend the standing of one's ancestors came the alarming possibility of steep social decline. When high-ranking men inherited their status in the medieval era, they faced little need to demonstrate individual excellence. But as social position became increasingly untethered from birth, men had to somehow prove themselves special and deserving of respect. Personal accomplishment became far more than just a window for escapism or intriguing intellectual positions. Individualism emerged as a central strategy for social success.

Of course, in spite of the rising stress on personal achievement, conformist Confucian ethics and the ritual canon retained considerable prestige. Some elite families assiduously upheld the old scholarship, staking a claim to superiority by virtue of their classical erudition. They continued to restrain themselves according to the old ritual standards. Nevertheless, far more people now valued individual emotion, belief, and attainment. Social mobility gave rise to the ideal of meritocracy, making individual accomplishment necessary for social success. Ultimately, a keen awareness of the potential uniqueness of the individual transformed virtually every aspect of Chinese culture.

These heady changes in views toward the individual constitute the background to the ascent of tea as a major cultural practice in China. Tea enjoyed increasingly wide appreciation during the cultural ferment of the Tang. And during the Song dynasty, as society underwent wrenching transitions, connoisseurs raised their sensibilities to a zenith of refinement. As tea became a fixture of daily life, not only had individualistic expression of ideas and feelings become laudable, but intense competition amid social mobility also made personal distinction a necessity for the ambitious. When tea became a newly popular addition to the quotidian routine, both the established elite and restless social climbers used it to amplify distinctions between themselves and others. In other words, tea served as an important medium for self-expression at a time when society began to emphasize individual merit and the elite used objects and practices to distinguish themselves. Poetry, calligraphy, painting, and scholarship constituted major achievements. But even minor accomplishments such as incense appreciation, gardening, and antique collecting could mark someone out as special. So the use of tea culture to create an individualistic persona does not represent an anomalous case. Instead it exemplifies a far wider trend of people marshaling material culture to take advantage of individualism's rising utility.

Each chapter of this book explores a different aspect of how cultured people engaged tea drinking to highlight their individual accomplishments and thus elevate their public image. The first chapter introduces the early rise of tea up to the time when a small number of insightful drinkers realized that it could serve as a vehicle capable of conveying profound meanings. The following section explores how tea unexpectedly became a way to express political power and cement relations among the powerful. Next comes a discussion of Lu Yu, unquestionably the most important figure in the history of Chinese tea. Although some predecessors had already begun to regard tea drinking as a refined practice that could be imbued with profound significance, Lu wrote a wildly successful book that popularized this provocative view. Largely as a result of his efforts, henceforth Chinese conventionally regarded tea as a highly cultured medium capable of articulating profound ideas.

The following chapters explore the various opportunities for individual expression provided by tea. A chapter on the rise of connoisseurship describes how some drinkers cultivated impressive expertise so that they could present themselves to their peers as exquisitely tasteful and refined gentlemen. Then an examination of how some fans took their admiration of this beverage even further by arguing that drinking tea correctly embodies the drinker's moral superiority. A corollary to this assumption implied that their own understanding of tea marked them as exceptionally virtuous. The following section explains how some drinkers abstracted the significance of tea even further by viewing it as an ingress to deep insights regarding religion and the natural world. This book concludes by exploring how some men used tea to lay claim to a superior form of manhood. The fact that a beverage could be coopted to express an elite style of masculinity demonstrates just how laden with cultural and social significance tea had become. When taken as a whole, this book sets forth the unexpected story of how the Chinese took an ordinary drink and made it into an expressive and supple means for conveying personal worth, thereby expressing a particular brand of individualism.

NOTES

1. Thomas M. Wilson, "Drinking Cultures: Sites and Practices in the Production and Expression of Identity." In *Drinking Cultures*, ed. Thomas M. Wilson (Oxford: Berg, 2005), 1–24.

2. Shen Songqin, "Liang Song yincha fengsu yu chaci," *Zhejiang Daxue xuebao* 31, no. 1 (2001): 75. Craig Clunas, *Superfluous Things: Material Culture and Social Status in Early Modern China* (Cambridge: Polity Press, 1991), 171 makes a similar argument about Ming dynasty China and early modern Europe, seeing both eras as witnessing "the invention of taste." In the case of tea culture, a highly sophisticated sense of good taste far predated the Ming.

3. Baldesar Castiglione, *The Book of the Courtier*, ed. Daniel Javitch (New York: W.W. Norton & Co., 2002), 22.

4. Jacob Burckhardt, *The Civilization of the Renaissance in Italy*, vol. II, trans. S. G. C. Middlemore (New York: Harper & Row, 1958), 361.

5. Burckhardt, *The Civilization of the Renaissance in Italy*, 303.

6. Yuan Jixi, *Renhai guzhou—Han Wei liuchao shi de gudu yishi* (Zhengzhou: Henan renmin, 1995).

7. Zhao Hui, *Liuchao shehui wenhua xintai* (Taipei: Wenjin, 1996), 1–106.

8. Joshua Fogel, *Politics and Sinology: The Case of Naitō Konan, 1866–1934* (Cambridge, MA: Harvard University Asia Center, 1984).

9. Nicolas Tackett, *The Destruction of the Medieval Chinese Aristocracy* (Cambridge, MA: Harvard University Asia Center, 2014).

I

THE RISE OF TEA

Although farmers usually clip back tea plants to form short bushes or long tidy hedges, wild tea trees grow to great heights. The cultivation of tea began so long ago that the tree's native range has been long forgotten. Botanists surmise that it originally grew somewhere in the remote mountainous subtropical region where the borders of China, Myanmar, and India converge. Mountains blocked glaciers from scraping across this area during the last ice age, a time when numerous species farther north suffered extinction, so it remains an unusual hotspot of biodiversity bursting with rare flora and fauna. Nationalistic scholars from China and India have tried to prove that this famous plant originated in what is now their country, but this is a sterile debate, as modern borders did not exist thousands of years ago when prehistoric peoples first began to exploit its leaves. Significantly, the tea tree comes from a place far from the heartland of Chinese culture. The natives of mountainous regions far to the south of historic China used tea first, gradually introducing it to areas farther north, so the integration of tea into Chinese culture took place gradually over the course of several centuries.

No testimonies survive to describe how and why people first consumed tea. While we now drink it as a beverage, most likely prehistoric hill tribes initially used tea leaves as food or herbal medicine. Ethnic minority peoples in Yunnan province and northern Myanmar still cook tea as a vegetable, often lightly fermenting the leaves to give the dish a pungent sour tinge. These modern preparations might have very ancient roots, preserving one of the earliest uses of tea. Tribal healers also probably employed tea for medicinal purposes. Even today the practitioners of both modern science and traditional Chinese medicine agree on the health benefits of tea drinking, and tribal shamans and herbalists probably explored these properties first.

Chinese first saw tea as an herbal tonic, crediting it with myriad health benefits. Physicians recommended it as a useful medicine that fosters longevity, cures drunkenness, prevents heatstroke, treats insomnia, induces relaxation, and of course quenches thirst.[1] Initially, Chinese treated tea as just another item in their extensive pharmacopoeia. People did not consume the leaves alone but used them as an ingredient in herbal mixtures, simmering various plants and foods together to produce a heady infusion. During the Tang dynasty, traces of this primal tea drinking continued to influence the palate, as drinkers still commonly steeped the leaves together with nuts, dried fruits, and other foods and spices. This ancient style of preparation has even survived down to the present with the so-called ground tea (*leicha*) consumed by the Hakka in some regions of China.[2]

The vagueness of early nomenclature bedevils any scholar searching for the beginnings of tea drinking. Initially Chinese did not even bother to give it a name of its own. Instead of creating a new character, they simply recycled an existing word and referred to it as *tu*, the name of a completely unrelated bitter herb that people in north China had consumed since antiquity.[3] Only when tea started to become common did someone bother to remove one stroke from the character *tu* and create the unique character *cha*, which still means tea in Mandarin. Because the earliest records refer to tea as *tu*, the name of a completely different plant, the initial inroads of tea into China have been irretrievably lost. Only after writers began referring to it by the unique name *cha* can we clearly trace its rise.

Because Chinese initially boiled this exotic southern herb together with other dried plants, the resulting healthful vegetable broth stood somewhere between medicine, food, and drink. Over time, people gradually came to view tea primarily as a beverage. Sanitation helps account for the welcome reception that tea received in China. In ancient times, Chinese most often drank water that had been boiled to render it sanitary. Over time, they realized that adding some tea leaves and other healthy flavorings to the pot would make tepid water taste far more agreeable.

Figure 1.1. The tea plant

Chinese originally regarded tea as an exotic drink, associating it with mysterious subtropical lands far to the south. By the third century, farmers were growing tea in China's far south and west, in what is now Yunnan, Guizhou, and Sichuan. After the fall of the Han dynasty, the culture of south China assumed unprecedented prominence. The violent invasion of northern China by nomadic peoples forced hordes of refugees southward, including many highly educated and prominent families. The focus of Chinese culture concurrently shifted south as well, putting the products and customs from this region in the spotlight. Tea still had an exotic image, and the air of exciting novelty helped spark interest in this bitter drink.[4] As farmers grew increasing amounts of tea, merchants exported surplus leaves to new markets, expanding the range of tea drinking.

In the third century, members of southern imperial courts embraced this new beverage, lending it considerable prestige. Interest at the apex of society drove producers and consumers to refine every aspect of tea, from production to drinking techniques. By the fourth century, tea began to infiltrate the lives of ordinary people throughout the south. A robust market led farmers to increase production and also create new hybrids suitable to a wider range of climates. And as growing and processing became increasingly sophisticated, a higher quality and more varied product emerged.[5] The appearance of many new types of tea appealed to a wider range of consumers, further stimulating demand.

People today would probably find this early tea almost unrecognizable. Whereas producers now process the leaves with dry heat, at first farmers steamed them. Also, modern tea usually consists of loose leaves, but originally producers packed the moist steamed leaves into a wooden mold to form them into a disk or some other shape.[6] Preparing this compressed tea for consumption required considerable time and effort. First the drinker (or a servant) cut off a piece of the tea disk and painstakingly ground it down into a fine powder with a mortar. Then they added hot water to the tea dust, usually together with some other flavorings, and waited for it to steep or simmer. Some of the hearty embellishments common in this era, such as scallions and ginger, would shock modern drinkers.

Tea did not conquer China's taste buds overnight. This bitter drink gradually spread northward, challenging and ultimately overturning traditional foodways. At the beginning of the Tang dynasty in the early seventh century, most Chinese still regarded tea as an exotic product from the outer margins of their empire. People in the north continued to resist this drink long after southerners had accepted it.[7] Tea only became common in the north, China's historical heartland and bastion of cultural orthodoxy, after the eighth century.[8]

Several larger trends encouraged the gradual spread of tea to north China.[9] Changing economic conditions played a particularly important role. The early medieval subsistence economy gradually gave way to commercial agriculture, allowing farmers to produce cash crops for sale on the open market. As more currency came into circulation, farmers realized that they could earn money by selling their crops instead of just growing grain for their own consumption. The market for all cash crops, from fruits to sugarcane, steadily expanded, making tea just one aspect of the far wider transformation of Chinese taste during the commercialization of agriculture.[10] As tea gained popularity, farmers produced ever larger quantities, allowing aggressive middlemen to push this product into new markets.

Simultaneous with the transformation of agriculture, consumer culture also underwent a major shift. The economy became increasingly complex and prosperous, providing more consumers with enough spare cash to buy this tasty subtropical herb. National unity and improving transportation links facilitated the shipment of tea to the north. The government also began to actively support tea drinking. Tea taxes provided welcome revenue, so authorities had good reason to encourage consumption. Tea parties and ceremonies at the imperial court also imbued the drink with cachet. Moreover, natural shifts in China's climate caused the average temperature to rise somewhat during the Tang era, making it easier for farmers to grow this subtropical plant in northern climes.

Subjective factors also spurred the rise of tea drinking. Buddhism gave tea a considerable boost.[11] Southern China is home to many of the most important temples and monasteries, so monks there had a chance to appreciate tea very early. Links between temples in different regions allowed southern monks to introduce tea to northern clergy. Southern literati also enthusiastically embraced tea drinking and wrote about their passion in poems, books, and essays, piquing interest among educated gentlemen in the north.[12]

From its marginal beginnings, tea drinking eventually became commonplace. Numerous records attest to the ubiquity of tea in daily life during the Tang and Song. People considered tea as common as "water and fire" and as necessary as soy sauce, cooking oil, and salt. Drinkers consumed it alone and in groups, on special occasions and as an everyday beverage, together with food and by itself between meals, in finely crafted vessels and rough pottery bowls. Guests expected their host to offer them tea as a standard token of hospitality. Tea could be found at every step of the social scale. From the eighth century onward, every emperor regularly drank tea, as did people of modest means. The popularity of tea even gave rise to new slang. For example, when a prostitute took too long to arrive, her customer might complain about "drinking cold tea" (*chi lengcha*).[13]

As this drink rose in popularity, teahouses spread throughout China. The earliest mention of venues dedicated specifically to tea drinking dates to the mid-Tang, the time when it became an everyday beverage.[14] Known by various names, teahouses became ubiquitous during the late Tang era.[15] As society prospered during the Song, these establishments became increasingly sophisticated. Some proprietors attracted customers by decorating the interior of their establishment with flowers and paintings. Musicians and singsong girls might entertain patrons, who could amuse themselves with cultured diversions such as the board game go (*weiqi*).[16] Authors of the time often set their stories in teahouses, attesting to the familiarity of ordinary people with these places.[17] Restaurants also served tea during meals, integrating this beverage into food culture.[18]

At the top of society, intense interest in tea gave rise to a culture of sophisticated connoisseurship. Erudite tea buffs wrote essays and entire books on the subject, exploring every aspect of production, processing, brewing, and appreciation in painstaking detail. Literati began drinking tea while practicing refined pursuits, fostering a civilized atmosphere to enhance their enjoyment of this drink. As a cult of connoisseurship developed, the styles of elite tea drinking diverged. In the palace, the emperor and his courtiers still used luxurious gold and silver tea wares and adhered to ostentatious rituals. In contrast, educated gentlemen increasingly preferred a low-key approach, often drinking tea with calculated ease and simplicity.

As tea became increasingly widespread, a dizzying number of new varieties came to market. The tea tree is easily hybridized, a trait that helps account for its success. Farmers adapted this subtropical plant to make it suitable to colder regions much farther north, and also to improve flavor, aroma, and other qualities. So as tea spread, the beverage became increasingly diverse.[19] During the Tang, ingenious producers created new cultivars and experimented with novel methods for raising the plants and processing the leaves. As a result of their efforts, extremely different kinds of tea could be found in a single region.[20] Faced with this plethora of new varieties, connoisseurs classified tea using increasingly fine distinctions. For example, they graded Jian'an tribute tea into thirty-eight types according to distinguishing features and quality, while imperial tea from Jianxi had thirty-two official varieties.[21]

The methods for processing and drinking tea steadily evolved, resulting in an increasingly delicate and satisfying drink. At the Tang court, officials formalized tea preparation and drinking into a daunting ritual. Although tea began as a humble vegetable broth cooked in the kitchen, the emperor and his circle now brewed it with gorgeous implements of precious metal and the finest ceramics. Of course most people made tea in a far simpler manner, although at the time preparing a proper bowl of tea always involved considerable effort. Paintings show guests enjoying dinner or engaging in refined pursuits while several servants busily carry out the complex business of tea preparation.

Tea drinkers usually wrapped compressed leaves in paper during storage, although the wealthy kept their tea in elaborate gold mesh containers. Either method protected the leaves from contamination by foreign elements while allowing contact with the air. Unlike the Song, when specialists considered an oxidized or fermented flavor undesirable, Tang connoisseurs appreciated the unpredictable complexity that results when the dried leaves interact with airborne microorganisms. After unwrapping the compressed block of leaves, the preparer cut off a piece and then slowly ground it down to a fine powder in a mortar. A thin elongated spoon could be used to scoop up the proper amount of powder and deposit it into a bowl. The drinker poured salted water from a ewer into the bowl, then waited patiently for the tea to infuse. At this point the powder might be beaten with a whisk to mix it into the liquid, speeding the brewing process and also producing surface foam that tea men considered attractive. Only after all of these preparatory steps had been completed could the drinker finally consume the finished decoction, swallowing the tea powder along with the briny liquid. Other than salt, which attested to tea's origins as a soup, Tang drinkers still routinely added strong flavorings such as scallion, ginger, dried citrus peel and berries, and various herbs.

Although this procedure seems dauntingly complex compared to modern methods of preparation, the average person brewed tea in a far simpler manner. While the elite had special tea wares, sometimes quite elegant and costly, most people used ordinary kitchenware to prepare tea, and they drank it from the same sort of bowls used to consume food. The primal beginnings of tea as an herbal soup made it amenable to being treated as a commonplace food in daily life. Because tea had two such different faces, either mundane or elegant depending on the context, it could readily accrue a rich array of connotations and cultural functions.

We can only speculate about how this medieval tea tasted. Unlike the modern product, Tang farmers processed it with steam instead of dry heat, and then compressed the wet leaves into dense disks. Oxidation might have given it a lightly fermented taste vaguely similar to modern oolong. However, because drinkers sucked down the tea powder along with the liquid, this powerful drink undoubtedly had a powerful flavor and noticeable caffeine kick. Saltwater and potent adulterants fortified the taste even further. The powdered tea (*matcha*) used in Japanese tea ceremony probably comes closest to Tang dynasty tea. Like its Tang prototype, Japanese still produce *matcha* by steaming the leaves, grinding them into a fine powder, infusing the tea and water in a large bowl, whipping the mixture into a foam with a whisk, and swallowing the ground tea along with the liquid. Even so, Tang Chinese used a different kind of leaf, salty water, and strong adulterants, all of which would have made Tang dynasty tea seem very foreign to a Japanese tea master. Were someone today transported back in time to taste a bowl of Tang dynasty tea, this intense salty brew of ground leaves flavored with scallions and ginger would likely strike the modern palate as much more akin to soup than what we now think of as tea.

Song dynasty drinkers consumed tea in a manner basically similar to their Tang predecessors. They still wrapped dried clumps of leaves in paper during storage. However, tastes had evolved, and people now regarded any changes in flavor and color as undesirable. To make the compressed leaves more stable during storage, it become common to seal the surface with a protective coat of vegetable oil, cutting off contact with the air. Leaves processed in this manner had to be soaked in water to remove the congealed oil, then carefully dried above a low fire. Toasting the leaves over a flame before grinding also helped eradicate any remaining traces of fermentation. Those who wanted to avoid the extra trouble of dealing with an oily shield would store their tea in

Figure 1.2. Ding ware bowl

airtight wooden containers. Some Song drinkers still added dried fruit peel and scallions to the drink, although authorities had begun to look down on this sort of adulteration and preferred to take their tea straight. Stripped of strong flavorings, this brew came much closer to what people today would recognize as tea.

As during the Tang, the average person avoided the complications willingly endured by aficionados. They simply spooned some powdered tea into a vessel containing hot water. After it had finished steeping, they then poured or ladled it into ordinary bowls for drinking. This streamlined mode of preparation marks the earliest precursor to the teapot. Although connoisseurs may have considered this simplified style of preparation woefully slapdash, it nevertheless became increasingly popular due to convenience.[22]

The formality of connoisseurship diminished during the Song era. Sumptuous drinking rituals went out of style, and even the emperor drank tea in a much more relaxed manner. Turning their backs on intricate vessels of gold and silver, literati now considered natural settings and humble materials tokens of good taste. Restraint rather than showiness revealed sophistication. Writings on the subject also evolved, assuming a less serious and formal tone. Literati often took a witty and playful approach to tea drinking, displaying greater confidence. By this time tea had become thoroughly assimilated into elite culture and so the refined gentleman now felt completely at ease with tea bowl in hand.

Why did Chinese elevate tea into such a significant cultural practice? One early boost came from the propensity to substitute tea in the numerous situations traditionally linked to alcohol, thereby borrowing the air of cultural importance traditionally associated with a long-established drink. Chinese have consumed alcohol since high antiquity and marked many important occasions by drinking beverages fermented from grain (technically a kind of ale, but conventionally translated into English as "wine"). When people met in groups, they often proclaimed an event's importance by consuming wine. The custom of consuming alcohol on special occasions imbued it with an aura of significance. For example, many ancient rituals featured alcohol, as people considered it the appropriate accompaniment for prestigious or virtuous activities. At the other extreme, idiosyncratic free thinkers such as Ruan Ji and Ji Kang indulged in wild drunkenness to symbolize their liberation from social constraints. The verses of famous poets such as Tao Qian and Li Bai depict "long drunk and never waking" as a deliberate strategy for releasing the creative temperament from mundane cares.[23]

Tea's usurpation of alcohol's traditional standing occurred during the Tang. At the beginning of the dynasty, wine still held the greatest cachet. Then as tea became popular, its fans began to use it in situations previously reserved for alcohol, challenging the prestige of the rival drink. A poem written for a popular audience entitled *Discussion on Tea and Wine* (*Cha jiu lun*), discovered among the documents recovered from the Dunhuang caves, wittily expresses the struggle for supremacy between these two beverages.[24] This satirical poem describes a comic debate between spirits personifying wine and tea, each claiming to be the better beverage. The spirit of water acts as judge. After hearing their competing pleas, water declares these rival drinks equally respectable and entreats them to exist in concord.

Opinions regarding the relative status of wine and tea seem to have changed surprisingly fast, undergoing a noticeable shift in the first half of the eighth century. Prior to that time, poets wrote mostly about wine. But in the second half of the eighth century, far more poems lauded tea.[25] This sudden swing in poetic subject matter reflects a broader change in elite taste, as people substituted tea for wine in many contexts. For example, parties and feasts began to feature tea instead of wine. Up to the Tang, gentlemen enjoyed cultured activities, such as listening to music or playing a board game, with a cup of wine in hand. Now they usually preferred tea. Song dynasty writers frequently portrayed wine as something ordinary and even mediocre while exalting tea as elegant and profound.

The copious poetic oeuvre of Bai Juyi (772–846) documents the transposition of wine and tea during the mid-Tang. Whereas the earlier poets Du Fu and Li Bai had famously praised wine while disregarding tea, Bai Juyi frequently wrote about both drinks, sometimes in the same poem, gradually tilting toward tea as the more worthy theme toward the end of his career.[26] Bai depicted tea in various ways, displaying an intimate familiarity with this drink and the culture enveloping it.[27] In some poems he mentions famous types of tea. Other verses describe technical details, including the processing of leaves and the mechanics of brewing. Laudatory poems emphasize the qualities that distinguish an outstanding brew.

In these poems, Bai identifies himself as an enthusiastic drinker who sipped tea morning, noon, evening, and even in the middle of the night. Sometimes he drank alone, feeling solitary and contemplative. On other occasions he imbibed it together with others, using tea as a focal point for social activities. He particularly enjoyed drinking tea in the company of other cultured gentlemen. Besides discussing literature during these sessions, they would also debate the merits of various kinds of tea and even the types of water best used to brew it. Bai Juyi did not simply dream up these incidents as a creative poetic conceit. Archaeologists have excavated some eight hundred fragments of tea ware from the site of his residence. These sherds include the remains of tea bowls, water jars, ewers, and the apparatus used to grind tea into a powder.[28] Bai Juyi unquestionably loved tea and made it part of his daily life.

A painting by the seventh-century Tang artist Yan Liben visually documents the substitution of tea for wine in the literati imagination. In this work the artist depicts a famous meeting of gentlemen that occurred in the year 353. Yan took his inspiration from an incident immortalized by the calligrapher and author Wang Xizhi (303–361) in his essay "Orchid Pavilion Preface" (*Lanting xu*), a milestone in Chinese literature whose influence cannot be exaggerated. Wang's brief but arresting work describes a conclave of talented scholars who amused themselves by floating wine cups down a winding stream. Whenever

Figure 1.3. Bai Juyi

one of the cups ran aground, whoever happened to be closest had to extemporize a poem. In this elegant essay, Wang does not merely describe this lighthearted occasion, but uses it as a starting point to muse about profound metaphysical questions, turning a cheerful afternoon outing into a pretext to ruminate about the fundamental nature of human existence. Many artists subsequently tried their hand at interpreting the scene described in this immortal essay. However, Yan Liben made a significant alteration by substituting tea for the original wine described by Wang Xizhi. Although this transposition might seem trivial, in fact it signals tea's usurpation of the privileged place held by wine in the imaginations of the educated.[29]

When gentlemen began to embrace tea drinking as a refined activity, they were immediately struck by the many parallels with wine, leading them to rapidly raise the standards of tea culture by mimicking the many sophisticated conventions already associated with the consumption of alcohol. Because literati had long associated wine with art and high culture, they treated tea in the same manner. For example, artists began to depict tea drinking as a way to graphically convey elegance, reclusion, deep thought, and other abstract ideals.[30] The long tradition of celebrating wine with poetry also found a counterpart in tea culture. As poets had long praised wine in verse, they began to write enthusiastically about tea. Wine served as a ready-made template for the new but increasingly important genre of tea poetry.[31]

Poets composed the earliest verses about tea in the *fu* genre, a style of prosody sometimes referred to in English as an ode. Han dynasty authors favored this verbose style, which used ornate and difficult language to celebrate exalted themes. Some Han dynasty *fu*, for example, detailed the luxury of the palace and grand imperial outings. Over time, however, poets applied this mode of expression to more intimate themes such as travel, emotions, and the natural world. During the early medieval era, as tea drinking increased in popularity, poets turned away from bombast to focus on more personal topics. This shift in focus made *fu* an appropriate medium for expressing ideas and feelings about tea. For example, the Western Jin dynasty poem "Picking Tea in the Evening" (*Chuan fu*), the first surviving literary work dedicated specifically to tea, already displays keen sensitivity toward the major aspects of tea production and appreciation. The author crafts an ode that lavishly describes beautiful tea fields, ceramic vessels, pure water, and even the attractive bubbles on the surface of a bowl of whipped tea.[32]

Tea poetry matured during the Tang. As bookish gentlemen embraced this beverage and refined their connoisseurship, they recognized tea as an appropriate theme for literature. Tea poetry became extremely popular during the mid-Tang, and about three-fourths of tea poetry from the period dates to the second half of the dynasty. Not only had this delicious herb become widely available, but tea buffs also regarded it as fundamentally different from other drinks. They elevated their favorite beverage into a profound topic of discourse worthy of detailed exploration. Poets also regarded tea as a fecund source of literary inspiration. They realized that sipping tea nurtures a contemplative disposition, and even believed that drinking tea causes verses to form spontaneously in the mind.[33] By the late Tang, the popularity of the *fu* genre had declined, so poets employed a variety of newly popular modes to write about tea. The diversity of genres provided poets with greater freedom to express their thoughts and feelings on the subject.[34] During the Song, tea poetry remained extremely popular. Increasing tea consumption, a flourishing commercial economy, the circulation of detailed books about tea, and changes in ideas about literature all boosted tea poetry toward ever loftier heights.[35]

As the aesthetics of tea drinking developed, connoisseurs devoted increasing attention to the vessels used to brew and consume it.[36] At first drinkers did not use specialized tea wares. Before people began to regard tea as a cultured drink, they just prepared it in the same vessels used for hot water and soup. But when gentlemen began to manipulate their tea drinking habits to express good taste, they increasingly valued appearance as well as practicality.

The aestheticization of tea ware gave rise to many kinds of containers. Tang courtiers favored the luxury of finely wrought pieces made from gold and silver. Most drinkers, however, used ceramic vessels. The Tang tea expert Lu Yu lists twenty-eight types of tea implements, attesting to the wide selection of equipage already available even in the early phase of connoisseurship. Tea vessels already encompassed a considerable range of styles during the Tang, ranging from unpretentious Changsha ware to elegant celadon Yue and white Ding. In addition to offering a variety of glazes, potters fashioned caddies, ewers, and bowls into specialized shapes. Many of the new forms of stoneware responded to problems encountered during tea preparation. For example, when servants brewed tea for the wealthy, they had to carry the hot drink from fire to table. Transporting bowls and ewers of scalding liquid presented a challenge that wine drinkers never faced. In response, potters devised clever new designs, such as resting the bowl inside a special holder that made it easy and safe for servants to transport hot liquid.

During the Song, potters crafted many of their finest vessels specifically for tea. As before, many tea bowls fit snugly into a specialized stand for easy carrying. Although simple white Ding ware remained fashionable, technological advances had made new glaze colors available. Tea vessels in purple Jun ware made a striking impression, while the emperor's circle often favored elegantly subtle Ru and Guan celadon. Many literati defied the trend toward technical perfection and instead sought out simple, austere, and interestingly imperfect tea wares. Jian ware bowls, usually known in English by the Japanese name *tenmoku*, initially gained popularity among connoisseurs in the tea powerhouse of Fujian. These unassuming black bowls, sometimes distinguished by interesting glaze drips and shiny surface patterns, embodied a new direction in elite culture, as gentlemen rejected the previous emphasis on luxury for a calculatedly simple aesthetic.

In this era loose-leaf tea first started to gain popularity, leading to momentous changes in drinking customs. At first people of limited

Figure 1.4. Tea bowl with stand

means had resorted to loose leaves as an economy measure. As long as drinkers ground the leaves down into a fine powder, which they sucked down along with the liquid, a batch of leaves could deliver only one infusion, making powdered tea both time-consuming to brew and relatively expensive to consume. For the wealthy, this extravagant drinking method posed no problem. But when tea became ubiquitous at all levels of society, less prosperous consumers demanded a cheap drink that they could brew quickly with little fuss. Loose leaves provided the solution. By abandoning grinding, drinkers could make their tea with ease. And they could sip this relatively weak liquid all day long without ill effect, extending their enjoyment. During the Song, loose leaves remained largely confined to the bottom rungs of society, but this new style of drinking gradually made its way up the social ladder, eventually becoming the norm.

This early loose-leaf tea probably tasted somewhat different from the current version due to the method of processing used at the time. Nowadays farmers use dry heat to cure loose leaves, but originally they prepared them as they always had and steamed the leaves. Steaming probably caused the tea to lose some potency. As long as drinkers sucked down the powdered leaves along with the liquid, the beverage had an extremely strong flavor. But when people brewed loose-leaf tea, they consumed only the liquid and discarded the used leaves. Moreover, as deliberate fermentation had not yet caught on, these leaves were probably green and mild. Although we will never know how this tea tasted, judged by today's standards it would probably have seemed fairly light.

The Yuan dynasty, spanning the late thirteenth and mid-fourteenth centuries, marked a key time of transition in the history of tea. The elite continued to favor expensive disks, as compressed tea maintained an aura of prestige. However, these luxury items became increasingly confined to a rarified group of connoisseurs. The average person now seldom came in contact with old-fashioned tea disks. Instead, consumers usually bought preground tea from merchants in the marketplace, much as Japanese today purchase *matcha* in powdered form. Buying powder instead of disks allowed drinkers to infuse tea in the traditional fashion without having to first grind down a hard clump of tea.

Although powdered tea remained common, loose leaves won over increasing numbers of consumers due to their undeniable convenience and low cost. The characteristics of loose-leaf tea also changed during the Yuan. To bolster flavor, farmers began to lightly toast the leaves over a flame after steaming. Once toasting had caught on, producers realized that steaming had become superfluous and tea could be processed using dry heat alone. Drying the leaves by tossing them around in a large wok imparted a rich full-bodied flavor, meaning that fewer leaves could brew a decent bowl of tea. By this time, farmers processed loose-leaf tea in essentially the same manner as today, and it probably had a flavor comparable to the green tea we now drink.

By the early Ming dynasty (1368–1644), tea took on a fully modern form. The dynasty's founder Ming Taizu came from poor peasant stock, so to him tea disks seemed completely alien. After he ascended the throne, he continued to drink the loose-leaf tea consumed by commoners. Moreover, this coarse ruler lacked exposure to the culture of tea

Figure 1.5. Ming dynasty teapot

and viewed it simply as a pleasant beverage. Taizu abolished the remaining tiresome court rituals associated with tea, preferring to consume it informally. From this time forward, from the apex of society down to the poor, with the exception of some anachronistic local oddities and ethnic customs, Chinese favored loose-leaf tea.

Ming drinkers simply steeped leaves in hot water using a small pot or covered cup. Brewing tea in a pot and then pouring the liquid into small cups has several advantages. The brewed tea stays warm much longer because it does not have to be transported from fire to table. And drinkers can maneuver dainty modern teacups far more easily than a capacious Tang dynasty tea bowl. A pot also concentrates the flavor, allowing rich tea to be brewed with a minimum number of leaves. The pots developed in the Ming would not seem unfamiliar to drinkers today, and potters of that era developed ingenious and beautiful designs. When people brewed dry-roasted loose-leaf tea in a ceramic pot, tea drinking reached its current form. Subsequent improvements have provided only minor refinements to Ming dynasty practices.

NOTES

1. Li Bincheng, "Tangren yu cha," *Nongye kaogu* 2 (1995): 25. This early view of tea influenced Lu Yu. He begins his famous work on the subject not by describing tea as a beverage but instead emphasizing its curative properties. Lu Yü, *The Classic of Tea: Origins & Rituals*, trans. Francis Ross Carpenter. (Hopewell, NJ: Ecco, 1974), 60–61; Lu Yu, *Cha jing jiaozhu*, annot. Shen Dongmei (Taipei: Yuhe Wenhua, 2009), 1:42–43.

2. Xue Qiao and Liu Jinfeng, "Woguo Han Tang cha wenhua de huo huashi—leicha," *Nongye kaogu* 2 (1995): 143–46.

3. For the history of the characters *tu* and *cha* see Zhu Zizhen, "Guanyu 'cha' zi chuyu zhong Tang de kuangzheng," *Gujin nongye* 2 (1996): 42–46; Chen Huanliang and Liang Xiong, "'Tu' 'cha' yitong kaolue," *Zhongshan Daxue xuebao* 4 (2002): 77–80. For ancient poems about *tu*, some of which might refer to tea, see Han Shihua, "Lun chashi de yuanyuan yu fazhan," *Zhongshan Daxue xuebao* 5 (2000): 59–63. For the origins and early history of tea see H. T. Huang, *Science and Civilization in China*, vol. 6: *Biology and Biological Technology*, part 5, *Fermentations and Food Science* (Cambridge: Cambridge University Press, 2000), 507–13 and James A. Benn, *Tea in China: A Religious and Cultural History* (Honolulu: University of Hawaii Press, 2015), 22–36.

4. E. N. Anderson, *The Food of China* (New Haven: Yale University Press, 1988), 67; Victor H. Mair and Erling Hoh, *The True History of Tea* (London: Thames & Hudson, 2009), 29–36.

5. Huang, *Science and Civilization in China*, vol. 6: *Biology and Biological Technology*, part 5, *Fermentations and Food Science*, 519–54 discusses in detail the changing ways that tea was processed.

6. Bret Hinsch, "Reconstructing a Lost Chinese Art: Molded Tea Leaves," *Asian-Pacific Culture Quarterly* 26, no. 2 (1998): 63–74.

7. E. N. Anderson, *Food and Environment in Early and Medieval China* (Philadelphia: University of Pennsylvania Press, 2014), 163.

8. Li Jing, "Da yunhe—Tangdai yincha zhi feng de beijian zhi lu," *Zhongguo shehui jingjishi yanjiu* 3 (2003): 49–50. Mair and Hoh, *The True History of Tea*, 40–56 summarize the history of tea during the Tang era.

9. Li Jing, "Da yunhe," 50–51.

10. Michael Freeman, "Sung," in *Food in Chinese Culture: Anthropological and Historical Perspectives*, ed. K. C. Chang (New Haven: Yale University Press, 1977), 146–48; Sun Hongsheng, *Tang Song chaye jingji* (Beijing: Shehui kexue wenxian, 2001).

11. Benn, *Tea in China*, 39–40, 55–68, 81–84, 86–90, 125–44.

12. Wang Shuanghuai, "Lun Tangdai yincha fengqi xingcheng de yuanyin," *Nongye kaogu* 4 (1998): 42.

13. Ding Chuan, *Songren yishi huibian* (Taipei: Taiwan shangwu, 1982), 13:662.

14. Liu Xuezhong, "Zhongguo gudai chaguan kaolun," *Shehui kexue zhanxian* 5 (1994): 120, 122.

15. Li Bincheng, "Tangren yu cha," *Nongye kaogu* 2 (1995): 16.

16. Liu, "Zhongguo gudai chaguan kaolun," 121; Zhu Zizhen, *Chashi chutan* (Beijing: Zhongguo nongye, 1996), 74–77.

17. Yang Zihua, "'Shuihu' yu Song Yuan Hangzhou de cha wenhua," *Yuanyang Shifan Gaodeng Zhuanke Xuexiao xuebao* 28, no. 2 (2008): 29–33.

18. Wu Zimu, *Mengliangu* (Taipei: Zhonghua, 1985), 16:142–44.

19. Zhang Zexian, "Han Tang shiqi de chaye," *Wenshi* 11 (1981): 61–79; Chen Qinyu, "Tangdai cha de shengchan yu yunxiao," *Gugong wenwu yuekan* 81 (1989): 110–25.

20. Li Hui, "Anhui Tangdai chaye gouchen," *Chizhou Xueyuan xuebao* 23, no. 4 (2009): 87–94. Mao Wenxi, *Chapu*, in *Zhongguo gudai chaye quanshu*, ed. Ruan Haogeng et al. (Hangzhou: Zhejiang sheying, 1999), 45–49, written during the Five Dynasties era between Tang and Song, lists a large number of teas classified according to region. This work attests that many places were producing a wide variety of teas at the time, and gives an impression of the immense diversity of teas that were available.

21. This classification system is described in the Song dynasty work Song Zian, *Dongxi shi chalu*, in *Zhongguo gudai chaye quanshu*, ed. Ruan Haogeng et al. (Hangzhou: Zhejiang sheying, 1999), 71–76.

22. Liao Baoxiu, *Songdai chichafa yu chaqi zhi yanjiu* (Taipei: Guoli Gugong Bowuyuan, 1996), 36–37.

23. Liu Xuezhong, "Cong jiu dao cha—gudai wenren de renge yanbian zongtan," *Fuyang Shiyuan xuebao* 4 (1995): 29.

24. James A. Benn, "Buddhism, Alcohol, and Tea in Medieval China," in *Of Tripod and Palate: Food, Politics and Religion in Traditional China*, ed. Roel Sterckx (New York: Palgrave Macmillan, 2005), 215–21; Benn, *Tea in China*, 44–51. For the complete annotated text see Wang Fu, *Cha jiu lun*, in *Zhongguo gudai chaye quanshu*, 39–44. Li Delong, "Dunhuang yishu 'Chajiulun' zhong de chajiu zhengsheng," *Nongye kaogu* 2 (1994): 72–77 discusses editions of the poem in Dunhuang documents S406, S5774, P2718, P2875, P2972, P3910. Using P2718 as the core text, this article provides a full transcription on pp. 72–73. Huang Yufeng, "Wan Tang zhi Song chu fojiao de cha jiu wenhua yanjiu—yi Dunhuang xieben 'Cha jiu lun' wei li," *Wenxuejie* 8 (2011): 99–101 argues that this poem should be seen in the context of the rise of Buddhism, which encouraged believers to abstain from alcohol.

25. Li Bincheng, "Tangren yu cha," 18.

26. Liu, "Cong jiu dao cha, 30.

27. The classification of Bai Juyi's tea poems into four types, together with examples of each class, is found in Zhou Shenghong, "Man ou si ru kan chi wan ying yuan wo shi bie charen: Bai Juyi chashi shuping," *Mudanjiang Shifan Xueyuan xuebao* 5 (2010): 40–45.

28. Liang Zi, "Bai Juyi guju chutu chaqi," *Nongye kaogu* 4 (1995): 84.

29. Song Houling, "Chahua, chahua," *Gugong wenwu yuekan* 4 (1983): 104.

30. Hu Dan, *Chayi fengqing: Zhongguo cha yu shuhua zhuanke yishu de qihe* (Beijing: Guangming ribao, 1999), 12–21.

31. Lin Jiali and Yang Jian, "Tang Wudai chashi de fazhan yanbian ji qi wenhua fengmao," *Zhejiang Shuren Daxue xuebao* 11, no. 4 (2011): 55.

32. Hou Ping, "Gudai chafu yanjiu," *Nongye kaogu* 2 (2011): 130.

33. Li, "Tangren yu cha," 19.

34. Shi Shaohua, *Songdai yong chashi yanjiu* (Taipei: Wenjin, 1996), 17; Hou Ping, "Gudai chafu yanjiu," 131; Lin Jiali and Yang Jian, "Tang Wudai chashi de fazhan yanbian ji qi wenhua fengmao," 52–57.

35. Shi, *Songdai yong chashi yanjiu*, 50.

36. Guo Danying and Chen Gang, "Song feng zhu lu jiancha—mantan Tangdai chaju," *Cha bolan* 8 (2009): 34–39; Wang Jianping, *Chaju qingya: Zhongguo chaju yishu yu jianshang* (Beijing: Guangming ribao, 1999), 5–51; Liao, *Songdai chichafa yu chaqi zhi yanjiu*, 40–99.

2

POWER

As an air of prestige steadily accrued to tea drinking, by the Tang dynasty this beverage had unexpectedly became a useful medium for expressing and bolstering power. Although China's elite embraced tea for a number of reasons, they particularly valued its capacity to manifest authority and status. Of course not everyone regarded this pleasant drink in such blunt terms, and many gentlemen tried to hold tea culture above the muck of politics and factional rivalry. In fact, many connoisseurs came to tea as a refuge, disgusted by cynical machinations in the halls of power. They used tea as an escape from grim reality, as a consolation for their complicity with an unpleasant system, or to assuage the wounds of a failed career. Nevertheless, tea had far more practical uses for those in positions of authority.

However much Chinese writers and artists have celebrated the otherworldly recluse, most well-placed men endeavored to maximize their own power and the authority of the institutions they served. Tea drinking provided these realists with one more tool in their arsenal. Appreciating how tea became a way to exercise power requires a broader view of imperial Chinese governance. In his classic analysis of politics, Max Weber famously asserted that the most basic foundation of power consists of a monopoly on the use of violence.[1] Yet as a political system evolves, those at the top need to develop more subtle methods for bolstering prestige and authority. Political symbols, rituals, customs, beliefs, and ideologies all become increasingly sophisticated over time. The ruling class cannot stay in power over the long term simply by issuing orders and physically punishing those who refuse to disobey. They have to discover how to persuade, attract, motivate, inspire, and awe. After many centuries of elaboration, China's political system had become extremely subtle, allowing tea to assume a role as an instrument of governance.

Because the elite relied so much on ceremony to manifest power, formalized tea drinking fit seamlessly into China's highly articulated body of political ritual. While every society uses ritual to display and reinforce power, in China this practice became unusually sophisticated. Influential thinkers pondered this subject since antiquity, developing a detailed theory of ritual that situated ceremonies within a larger ethical framework. Ritual initially assumed prominence in Chinese political discourse as a response to chaos. Confucius and other Eastern Zhou (770–256 BCE) thinkers addressed the unending war and wrenching changes plaguing their societies and tried to pose workable solutions. Confucius argued that society could be stabilized and even improved if people act in accordance with the standardized templates of ethical behavior set down in the ritual canon. Sometimes a ceremony explicitly acts out a particular virtue, demonstrating proper standards of conduct. Yet even arbitrary prescribed behavior can foster stability by standardizing social intercourse.

Benjamin Schwartz helpfully defines the Chinese rites (*li*) as standard ceremonies, manners, and behavioral norms that "bind human beings and the spirits together in networks of interacting roles within the family, within human society, and with the numinous realm beyond."[2] While ancient theorists initially expressed ritual theory in general terms, over time a group of dedicated specialists edited together lengthy compendia that provided specific guidelines for conducting ceremonies. By the Tang, although educated gentlemen rarely practiced most of these archaic procedures, many influential thinkers nevertheless continued to regard the ritual canon with awe, seeing it almost akin to holy writ.

This rich body of theory and practice established the intellectual framework for the ritualization of tea. During the Tang, tea drinking became insinuated into court ceremonial. Most visibly, emperors employed tea in religious rituals such as sacrifices to the gods and ancestors. Since distant antiquity, Chinese had regarded water as far too humble for conducting religious rites, so they employed alcohol to mark the sacred. Rulers of the Shang dynasty (ca. 1600–1046 BCE) made alcohol a standard component of state rituals, dedicating a majority of their precious bronze vessels to preparing, serving, and drinking fermented brews. People of the Zhou dynasty (1046–256 BCE) upheld this custom, and alcohol remained a standard component in the state worship of ancestors and major deities up through the early medieval era.

Beginning in the Tang, however, state ritual underwent a major shift. In reaction to the general displacement of wine by tea in society at large, state sacrifices began to feature this new drink as well.[3] In light of the political importance of these rites, this substitution had profound implications. Most importantly, rulers conducted ceremonies to display their unique connection with the supernatural, thereby legitimizing their reign. Ever since the Bronze Age, these profound rituals had employed alcohol. Substituting tea for wine elevated this new beverage, which until recently had been regarded as extremely humble, into an important tool for sanctifying the highest reaches of political power.

Once tea assumed a place among the most sacred political rituals, it seemed a fitting fixture for other aspects of court life as well. Most visibly, tea became a standard gift from the emperor to his favorites as a sign of partiality. The political system of imperial China illustrates anthropologist Marcel Mauss's famous assertion that a gift is rarely free, as it usually functions as a material token in a system of reciprocal exchanges that strengthens social bonds.[4] Participants in this network expected the recipient of a gift of tea to feel a sense of obligation that he could repay by demonstrating loyalty to the throne.

Because gift giving strengthened the bonds between ruler and ruled, since remote antiquity Chinese sovereigns had routinely handed out valuable items to key personages. In the absence of strong institutions during ancient times, gift giving eased the conduct of administration by forging strategic alliances. During the Bronze Age, when rulers had relatively few tools to enforce their will, gifts bolstered their authority. And over the following centuries, even as the system of government developed and rulers gained more direct ways to control personnel, emperors continued to generously hand out gifts. A present from the emperor, however mundane, conferred immense prestige on the recipient, generating a sense of obligation that nurtured loyalty and obedience. The utility of gift giving allowed it to remain a mainstay of China's political system even as institutions evolved in complexity and efficacy.

Regular gifts of tea from the ruler to officials, relatives, and favorites not only bolstered the ruler's public image by symbolizing his generosity, but also elevated the recipient, who could proudly flaunt a token of imperial largess. The sociability of tea drinking provided numerous opportunities to show off a gift from the emperor. Moreover, tea leaves could be easily subdivided and parceled out as secondary gifts, allowing the well connected to emphasize their connection with the throne. In a society obsessed with reputation, showing off a symbol of the emperor's esteem carried significant cachet.

Of course, those who obtained this impressive status symbol felt inclined to reciprocate by supporting the bestower of such a prestigious item. Given the fragility of the central government throughout most of the Tang, emperors compensated for the limits of their authority within this fissile system by handing out gifts of tea to influential figures. Human beings staff the supposedly faceless institutions of government, and they can be swayed by subjective emotional appeals. Tang emperors understood the human factor of politics and strove to build up personal bonds with important decision makers. Gifts of tea thus became a workable strategy for the emperor to boost his power.

Tea became imbricated into almost every aspect of court life. For example, the dowries of women in the imperial clan included large amounts of fine tea, impressing in-laws with imperial wealth. Almost every activity of the imperial circle and high officialdom included tea drinking. Hosts served this drink to their guests, the faithful sipped it when visiting temples, and high-ranking spectators drank tea while observing martial arts displays and other entertainments.[5] Tea featured at various court feasts, both serious occasions and carefree celebrations accompanied by music and poetry recitation.

The elaborate festivities marking the Qingming ancestral sacrifices exemplify how the Tang court drank tea in a manner so formal that it assumed the tone of a solemn ritual. The Qingming ceremonies presented the emperor with a valuable opportunity to bolster his power. By ostentatiously demonstrating regard for his ancestors, the ruler cultivated an aura of piety and seriousness, reinforcing his public image and increasing the reach of his influence. As befitted a major court ritual, participants used the finest tea wares wrought from precious metals, elaborately worked by the most skillful craftsmen. The emperor and his court did not freely quaff this drink, but consumed it with deliberation in a highly ritualized manner. First, servants burned incense to purify the air and evoke an otherworldly atmosphere. Then they presented the tea caddy to the ruler and dramatically opened it, displaying the compressed leaves for his approval. Next they brought out an array of gorgeous tea wares and showed them to the ruler and courtiers, who expressed their admiration. After lightly toasting the leaves over a flame to rid them of any odd tastes and odors, the audience examined them and assessed their quality. Favored officials composed poetry to celebrate this sublime tea, reciting their verses for the enjoyment of the assembled court. Only after this elaborate prelude did servants finally grind the leaves down to a powder, steep it in hot water, and present the finished drink to participants for consumption.[6] This daunting ritual was not unique to the Qingming festivities. Other important religious and ritual occasions at court featured similar ritualistic tea drinking. For example, an equally elaborate tea feast marked the conclusion of a religious sacrifice held at the Tang court in 798.[7]

Tea continued to play a significant ceremonial role during the Song dynasty, when rulers used it in court rituals such as the *shixue,* held to celebrate education and literature. By ostentatiously patronizing learning, the ruler associated himself with the academic pursuits that China's elite held in supreme regard, thereby elevating his own reputation by association. For this rite the emperor personally visited the Grand Academy (*taixue*) to venerate the memory of Confucius and pay his respects to the teachers in residence. After listening to an erudite scholar explicate a token passage from the classical canon, the ruler, officials, and academics would all drink tea together.[8] Originally this ceremony featured alcohol, but during the Southern Song participants drank tea instead, an indication of how tea steadily superseded alcohol in official ritual.

The insinuation of tea into the heart of court life led Chinese to consider it an ideal gift for presentation to foreign rulers. Emperors often presented symbolic gifts of tea to key allies, such as the rulers of Tibet. As with domestic gifts of tea to powerful officials, presenting high-quality tea to a foreign ruler symbolized the emperor's personal largesse while elevating the position of the recipient in the eyes of his own people. Moreover, encouraging powerful foreign leaders to take up tea drinking expanded China's cultural influence. In this early example of soft power, Chinese sought to expedite their relations with outsiders by Sinicizing foreign elites. If the lifestyles of foreign rulers altered to conform more closely to Chinese norms, potentially troublesome foreigners would become easier to understand and manage. The custom of presenting tea to foreign rulers continued for the rest of imperial history, reaching an apex during the Ming dynasty when gifts of tea became an important component of China's diplomatic strategy. The regular gifts of tea from Ming emperors to a wide range of religious authorities in Tibet, with the intent of "using tea to manage the barbarians" (*yi cha yu fan*), demonstrated their faith in this strategy.[9]

Even during the Tang, officials had already begun to employ tea as a diplomatic tool to smooth China's interactions with the outside world. Sometimes two sides exchanged tea as a formal courtesy. When Emperor Tang Taizong sent one of his daughters to marry the ruler of Tibet, thus cementing a diplomatic alliance, the Tibetans presented China's monarch with a large quantity of Tibetan-style tea as part of the betrothal gift. When the Chinese sampled this exotic tea they discovered to their surprise that they enjoyed it, initiating a courtly fad for drinking tea in the Tibetan style.[10]

Because tea had become an integral fixture of daily life at the imperial court and a routine gift to China's ministers and foreign potentates, the state required huge quantities of the finest possible leaves. The emperor could not simply purchase his tea on the open market, as merchants could not provide such huge quantities of a uniformly high-quality product. Moreover, consuming the same sort of tea available to any vulgar parvenu would rob the ruler of an opportunity to demonstrate his unique position in society. For tea to symbolize imperial power, it had to be made exclusive. As a result, the emperor deliberately monopolized the finest teas and doled them out as a mark of favor, using this largesse to demonstrate his authority and build useful connections. In response to these unique demands, a complex bureaucracy arose that could provide large quantities of imperial tea while guaranteeing unparalleled quality and exclusivity. The government established official posts to oversee the growing, processing, and delivery of "tribute tea" (*gongcha*) to the court.

Government agencies had produced specialized goods for rulers since the beginning of recorded history. During the Shang dynasty, when currency had not yet been invented and the simple economy could not support much commerce, the elite had no choice but to oversee the manufacture of all the luxuries necessary to maintain their unique way of life and mark their superior status. Workshops in the Shang capital produced special luxury items from a range of materials, including pottery, bone, bronze, and jade. The location of these workshops near the center of power allowed the king and nobility to oversee production and ensure that these special goods suited their taste. Due to the primitive economic conditions of the time, rulers had to use their authority to procure raw materials, including large quantities of ore and rarities such as cowry shells and turtle scapula, and have them transported long distances to the capital.

Even as China's economy matured and merchants emerged in large numbers, the government remained intimately involved with the design and production of court luxuries. The ruler and those around him enjoyed lofty status, distinctive duties, and an exceptional lifestyle. In consequence, they needed many goods unobtainable on the open market. Therefore the court needed to manage the production of some luxury items. For example, during the Han dynasty, palace ladies produced some of the matchlessly rich fabrics used to make the emperor's clothing. Empresses and empresses dowager visited this special workshop on the palace grounds to monitor this painstaking labor; sometimes they even participated in the work themselves.[11]

By the Tang, government procurement of articles for the court had evolved into a highly sophisticated "tribute" (*gongxian*) system, under which the palace bureaucracy acquired special textiles, foodstuffs, herbal medicines, animals, handicrafts, and other items from every part of China and the surrounding regions.[12] The government considered these tribute goods so vital that even during times of natural disaster, famine, or epidemic, when taxation normally eased, local officials still had to continue providing them. Not only did the court need these special goods to maintain the ambiance of luxury that reflected the ruler's position, but requiring subjects to provide tribute also attested to the emperor's sovereignty. According to the reasoning of people at the time, exacting tribute goods proved someone to be an emperor.

Under the tribute system, districts throughout China provided their local specialties to ensure that the court could enjoy the very best products from each part of this vast empire. Because China sprawls over such a wide range of climates and ecologies, each region could offer the palace unique items. Sometimes designated officials purchased a local specialty on the open market and sent it off to the capital. Other officials oversaw manufacturing directly to ensure suitable quality for the ruler and his entourage. Moreover, exotic goods from distant foreign lands arrived at court irregularly as gifts brought by embassies. Due to the difficulty of transporting goods long distances, often over poor local roads, officials also had to arrange shipping and ensure that the tribute items arrived at the capital intact and on time. After receiving a shipment of tribute articles, palace staff examined them and deposited each item in the appropriate warehouse.

This elaborate tribute bureaucracy long predated the rise of tea drinking. So when fine tea became necessary for emperors to maintain their distinctive lifestyle, officials simply added it to the existing system. In doing so, the government took on the task of growing and processing tea of the highest possible quality. Tang tribute officials established the first large tribute tea factory in the year 770 at Mt. Guzhu in what is now Zhejiang province. That region and the surrounding area produced a highly regarded tea known as "purple shoots" (*zisun*).[13] Officials sent in small amounts of this tea as tribute in the early years of the dynasty. When this variety of tea came into favor, the court began to demand vast quantities annually. Eventually purple shoots became so desirable that the ruler dispatched an official from the central government to oversee its production, and prime fields came under government ownership. Officials oversaw the production of huge amounts of this premium product. In just one year, tribute officials sent in 18,408 catties of Purple Shoot tea to the capital.[14] Apparently tribute officials succeeded in crafting a superb product, as the connoisseur Lu Yu mentions it approvingly as one of the finest teas.

Government functionaries closely supervised the processing of "officially baked" (*guanbei*) tea, which referred to tea leaves dried and processed under government supervision. To maintain the highest quality, tribute officials did not entrust slaves or convicts with the most critical aspects of production. Instead, skilled farming households and experienced workers processed this tea under the watchful eyes of tribute officials. Government supervision ensured that farmers and workers would be held to the highest standards of quality in growing, harvesting, and producing the final product. This system quickly grew on an im-

Figure 2.1. Song dynasty imperial tea disk

pressive scale. Some surviving inscriptions from a Tang tribute tea processing site have allowed scholars to reconstruct some of the particulars of this early tea tribute network.

Just one of the tribute tea bureaus set up in the Tang had more than thirty rooms. It employed thirty thousand corvée laborers and more than a thousand experienced tea workers.[15] Given the scale of these enterprises, not surprisingly the tribute system produced huge quantities of premium tea. And in addition to tribute tea produced under official supervision, skilled farmers also produced so-called people's tribute (*mingong*) tea. Although the tribute bureaucracy did not manage the growing or processing of this product, officials nonetheless deemed these leaves to be good enough to present to the emperor.

Brewing the best possible tea requires more than just exceptional leaves. The palace also had to locate a supply of good-tasting water to provide the ideal background for the spectrum of subtle flavors released by steeping leaves. To acquire water good enough for brewing the emperor's tea, tribute officials conferred with experts on the matter. Eventually courtiers declared water from the Jinsha spring in Huzhou particularly ideal for tea making. Once a spring had been identified as suitable for providing tribute water (*gongshui*), workers poured this precious liquid into silver bottles and dispatched regular shipments to the capital.[16]

Given the immense quantity of tribute tea produced each year, of course the emperor consumed only a tiny fraction of it himself. He parceled out almost all of these precious leaves to officials and favorites. Detailed rules regulated routine grants of tea leaves to high officials, imperial relatives, and foreign rulers. In addition to these predictable disbursements, however, the ruler also handed out special gifts at his pleasure. Receiving an unexpected allotment of tribute tea expressed the emperor's special regard, thereby symbolizing high social standing. So by handing out gifts of tea, the ruler could single out his favorites, instantly elevating the status of the lucky beneficiary.

During the Song dynasty, a large and sophisticated government apparatus continued to grow, produce, grade, and transport tribute tea.[17] The system for distributing tea to officials and favorites resembled that of the Tang in most respects, and tea drinking marked many of the occasions in court life. The poems of Emperor Song Huizong, many of which describe tea drinking, attest to the importance of this beverage at court and the aura of elegance that enshrouded it.[18]

As before, the court continued to source tea from Guzhu. However, tastes had become more cosmopolitan, so officials had to fan out over a much wider area to provide the emperor with a more diverse range of teas. As the tribute tea system steadily expanded in both area and output, some regions began to produce immense quantities of leaves for the court. Tribute officials oversaw the production of more than 500,000 catties annually in Huoshan, 400,000 catties in Shangcheng, 300,000 catties in Guangshan, and so on.[19] Under this system, the production of superb tea became an important goal of government. During the Song, about half of the tea producing regions in China sent in tea for imperial tribute.[20]

Interest steadily turned away from Purple Shoot in favor of other varieties. Increasingly tribute officials saw the Northern Garden (Beiyuan) in Jian'an (modern Jianping), located in a mountainous region of Fujian, as the source of the best tea.[21] In 1995 archaeologists excavated a Song dynasty site in what used to be the Northern Garden that had been used to process tribute tea, confirming the accuracy of contemporaneous records on the matter.[22] Although tea from this area had not yet attracted notice when Lu Yu composed his classic treatise on the subject, during the Song it became the most respected appellation by far. Numerous Song authors praised the quality of Fujian teas, and that region has maintained its reputation to the present. Today Fujian still produces the most expensive and highly regarded teas in China.

The tribute system had a major impact on how the Tang and Song elites perceived tea. Besides providing vast quantities of tea to the central government for distribution to officials and imperial favorites, thus guaranteeing this beverage a prominent position in the cultural life of those at the top of society, the tribute system also brought many officials into direct contact with tea production. A stint in the tribute tea bureaucracy informed the poetry and connoisseurship of many educated gentlemen, as this posting gave them an unusually intimate connection with tea. For example, for a time the famed litterateur Ouyang Xiu (1007–1072) supervised tribute tea production in Yangzhou. His tea poetry not only describes emotional resonances evoked by the drink, but also demonstrates a detailed technical knowledge that clearly reflects his practical experience in the tea bureaucracy.[23] Those who had served in the tribute system did not see tea merely as a dried disk sitting on a shelf or hot liquid steaming in a bowl. Managing tea production had given them an intimate bond with this drink, and many acquired a profound appreciation of its subtleties. The meticulous perfectionism of tea connoisseurship owes an enormous debt to the attentive officials who strove to make tea worthy of the emperor of China. They transmitted the highly specialized knowledge they had acquired through poems, essays, and friendly conversation.

Tea poetry from this period sometimes reflects the author's personal experiences while serving as a tea tribute official. Some poets looked back on their work managing tea production, describing specific scenes and emotions they recalled from their time overseeing tribute tea fields. The integration of technical details into poetry influenced the genre's conventions. For example, even poets who had not served in the tea bureaucracy sometimes mentioned the natural environment of tea fields and processing facilities. Readers enjoyed these details and had become accustomed to thinking about tea from the perspective of producer as well as consumer.

Many Song tea poems written by officials in charge of tribute tea describe mountain fields at dawn, a stereotypically beautiful scene that projects the elegance of a bowl of tea onto the natural world. During harvest season, tribute officials journeyed out into the fields very early in the morning to oversee picking, making sure that harvesters selected only the very best and most tender leaves. People of the time believed that tea leaves picked early in the morning had the finest flavor, so tea pickers had to start work before dawn and ceased at sunrise. Then as now, the spring flush usually yielded the best tea. Some poems stress the fact that the emperor's tea had to be picked before dawn to ensure optimum flavor. Because harvesting often took place early in the morning in the spring, when mountain regions were still quite cold, poets mention braving the morning chill while looking out over a verdant vista of beautiful tea fields at the crack of dawn.[24]

By requiring farmers to harvest tea early in the morning, large numbers of pickers sometimes swarmed over the narrow mountain trails as they struggled to finish their work before the sun rose too high and the supervising official called an end to the day's work.[25]

> Throngs tussle, trampling new moss.
> I turn my head toward first blush over the dragon's field.
> A warden beating a gong to urge haste,
> they carry baskets of tea down the mountain.
> When picking tea,
> one is not allowed to see the sunrise.

This poem by Xiong Fan, a Southern Song tea expert, does not depict tea from the standpoint of drinkers at the imperial court. The emperor and those around him only experienced tribute tea in its finished form, as dried leaves in a compressed disk. In contrast, Xiong assumes a far broader perspective. To him, tribute tea evokes the gorgeous mountain landscapes where busy farmers labor in the chilly morning air to produce this luxurious product. This poem transports the reader far from the capital to gaze out over remote mountain fields. The lively images of trampled moss and rushing feet contrast starkly with the air of serene dignity associated with drinking tribute tea. Rather than accepting the usual image of the emperor's tea as a token of ceremony and luxury, the poet surprises the reader by portraying it through his own personal experience with the early morning harvest.

Poetry also reveals how educated gentlemen steadily elevated tea into a locus of sustained reflection on the subjective nature of individual experience. During the Tang, courtiers usually appreciated tribute tea in staid groups adhering to ponderous ceremonial. In that era, the highest form of tea appreciation emphasized externalities, creating an awe-inspiring façade of grandiosity, luxury, privilege, and decorum. But as tea gained cultural significance, thoughtful drinkers engaged with this drink in increasingly subjective and intimate ways. Tea appreciation did not have to be public and orthodox; personal experiences in low key settings could be just as meaningful. Exploring the subjective side of tea empowered the individual by admitting room for distinctive experiences outside the realm of communal rites.

The ways courtiers used tea to project an image of authority, thereby bolstering their charisma and prestige, shifted significantly over time as tea culture gained sophistication. Originally they sought prestige by wallowing in an unabashed pursuit of luxury. Those around the emperor stored, brewed, and drank tea in precious vessels, often made of finely wrought gold or silver. Ritualized tea entertainments flaunted the emperor's lavish lifestyle in a grandiloquent fashion. Archaeologists have recovered a remarkable trove of opulent court tea wares from a pagoda at the Famen Temple, a vast Buddhist complex built in the capital. Famen thrived under imperial patronage, eventually expanding into a rambling series of buildings set around twenty-four courtyards. In 1987 authorities opened the underground treasury beneath a surviving sixth-century pagoda and discovered, among other riches, an extensive set of stunningly crafted Tang era tea wares. Given the sumptuousness of these objects, and their congruity with descriptions of imperial tea wares in written records, it seems certain that emperors had used them in court tea drinking ceremonies.[26]

Despite the showiness of this impressive array of silver and gold, the Famen tea wares perfectly suited the task at hand. For example, a tea caddy woven out of precious metal let the leaves breathe, allowing them

Figure 2.2. A feast with tea

to oxidize and develop a more complex flavor. However, in humid weather it would have been safer to store leaves in an airtight container. A silver box in the shape of a tortoise (symbolizing longevity), equipped with a tight-fitting lid, would have kept about half a kilo of tea leaves safely elevated and protected from the air and moisture. A mortar and wheel used to grind the leaves into fine powder shines with ornate gilt decoration. As Tang drinkers still added salt, spices, and other flavorings to the water along with the tea leaves, this set includes a richly ornamented plate to hold these adulterants during the ritualistic formalities of preparation. Craftsmen even used silver to construct the stove used to boil the tea water.

Turning tea drinking into a flamboyant display shows how much the Tang elite embellished this formerly humble custom to highlight their authority and prestige. As tea had become commonplace, consuming it instead of water or alcohol garnered no esteem in itself. But because most people still made and drank tea in a simple manner little different from consuming soup, to prepare it with delicately worked gilt implements and drink with elaborate politesse elevated one above the hoi polloi. Luxurious tea drinking became a vehicle for expressing status and power. It was never sufficient to simply *be* powerful. To be taken seriously and demand maximum deference, China's elite expressed their authority by creating a unique lifestyle. Drinking tea in such a sumptuous fashion proved their high rank and reinforced their supremacy.

This exceedingly luxurious style of tea drinking gradually declined in popularity. The decline of the medieval nobility and rising economic dynamism stimulated social mobility, altering the nature of elite status. In the past, when people looked to genealogy to determine rank, the elite did not have to prove their supremacy. They merely displayed it. An opulent style of tea exhibited the drinker's status, rightfully theirs as a birthright. But increasing social complexity put inherited status in doubt. Instead of simply showing off hereditary position, the elite had to somehow prove themselves superior to others. For this reason, high-placed drinkers increasingly preferred to sip tea while engaging in cultured activities to display their prestige.

As hereditary privilege decayed during the twilight of the Tang, connoisseurs began to look down on opulent tea rituals. In fact, some literati even wrote poems criticizing the loutishness of those who used tea to show off their wealth. Tasteful tea men increasingly assumed a subdued style, often emphasizing natural simplicity and a spirit of otherworldliness. Besides taking aim at vulgarity, their criticism of affected manners also conveyed implicit social criticism. Valuing gold and silver over morality and spirituality betrayed a clear lack of cultivation. Lavish tea wares also seemed to embody the louche self-indulgence denounced by the ancient authors of the Confucian classics. While the powerful saw opulent tea drinking as a way to express their authority, moralistic critics began to spurn it as dangerous decadence. Those in power eventually heeded these criticisms. Instead of obsessing over precious materials, elaborate workmanship, and grand rituals, court tea drinking increasingly imitated the conventions of educated gentlemen, taking skill and learned connoisseurship as supreme expressions of good taste. By imitating literati tea drinking, the emperor and his courtiers continued to display their prestige and status, albeit in an extremely different manner than before.

The shift toward connoisseurship in court tea drinking had already begun during the Tang dynasty, initially coexisting with lavish conspicuous consumption. The urbane Emperor Xuanzong (r. 712–756), whose reign marked a high point for Tang culture in many respects, not only enthusiastically consumed the drink but also took pride in his adroitness at tea preparation. While official court ceremonial still demanded sumptuous formality, behind closed doors Xuanzong enjoyed playing tea drinking games with his concubines. He especially liked whipping tea with a whisk in the style favored by literati, and his concubines would compete to see who could prepare a bowl of tea with the most attractive foam on top.[27] Although whipped tea had initially gained popularity among gentlemen connoisseurs, the emperor's adoption of this style of drinking helped popularize it further. By stressing skill at tea preparation and preparing it under highly exacting but relatively informal circumstances, court tea drinking became a more individualistic way to express high cultural status. This relaxed atmosphere also provided opportunities for officials and favorites to display their mastery of technique and arcane tea knowledge.

Emperor Wenzong (r. 827–840) also held informal tea drinking sessions amid the privacy of the inner reaches of the palace. An unusually cultivated monarch, he enjoyed reading and discussing literature in his spare time. Wenzong ordered palace ladies to prepare tea for the participants in his cultured salons. Matching tea with the written word brought the full spirit of literati tea drinking to court. Instead of stately rites, Wenzong paired tea with intellectual endeavors. Even in the cynosure of power, tea drinkers had increasing opportunities to show off their refinement and good taste.

This burgeoning culture of connoisseurship continued to develop for the remainder of the Tang. For example, Emperor Daizong (r. 762–779) also enjoyed tea. He even met the famed expert Lu Yu, whom he summoned to court to teach tea making to the nation's elite. Daizong's decision to bring the most advanced tea connoisseurship to the palace, considered a bastion of cultural orthodoxy, elevated Lu Yu's reputation and allowed him to publicize his carefully considered ideas about tea drinking. In welcoming the gentlemanly mode of tea to the court, Daizong veered even further from the calculated extravagance of the early Tang emperors. Individual discernment continued to displace mere cost, becoming the most prestigious way to drink tea.

In embracing the literati style of tea drinking, these emperors rejected courtly traditions for far more humble customs. As a cultural strategy, at first glance this apparent slide down the social scale might seem odd. While no one could possibly outdo the emperor of China in terms of sheer luxury, the monarch could never claim to be the most erudite or cultivated person in his empire. Yet discarding empty opulence in favor of literati-style connoisseurship acknowledged changes in elite culture at large. The elite increasingly ranked individualistic expressions of sophistication and discrimination above empty extravagance. A new view of the ideal person as a distinctive individual transformed tea culture even at the highest reaches of society.

The movement toward connoisseurship at court continued during the Song dynasty, when tea drinking reaching an apex of refinement. The book *Discussions of Tea in the Daguan Reign Era (Daguan chalun)*, written by Emperor Song Huizong (r. 1100–1126), attests to the impressive refinement of court tea drinking at the end of the Northern Song. It seems hard to believe that an emperor writing in his spare time could compose such an assured and insightful textbook on tea connoisseurship, one of the best works on the subject ever written. Emperor Huizong, perhaps the most artistically talented and tasteful ruler in China's long history, took tea very seriously, regarding it as far more than just an ordinary beverage. He believed that the way someone

Figure 2.3. Emperor Song Huizong

consumes tea discloses the drinker's innermost taste and character. In other words, tea drinking puts personal qualities, normally hidden from view, on public display. When consumed properly, the drinker exposes stylishness and even virtue, while clumsiness reveals personal flaws. This viewpoint made tea virtually synonymous with a person's fundamental nature.

Huizong believed that drinking tea properly requires more than simply adhering to standardized rituals or using fancy wares. The drinker must also acquire considerable knowledge about the various types of tea, down to the level of specific details about how each type is grown and processed. Although this information might not seem immediately relevant, Huizong believed that familiarity with the origins of each tea enriches a drinker's experience. Even relatively arcane knowledge about tea production thus became integrated into aesthetic practice. For example, Huizong wrote at length on the so-called dragon and phoenix tribute tea disks produced for the court.[28] He declared tea disks from Fujian the best, attributing their superlative quality to that region's unique climate.[29] His opinions became the standard judgment on the matter, and even today many experts place Fujian teas at the top of their rankings.

The imperial turn from mindless luxury to connoisseurship influenced how the emperor and his courtiers drank tea. In imitation of literati conventions, courtiers rejected gaudy vessels made of precious metals. Instead they consumed tea in an increasingly muted fashion, using exquisitely crafted yet deceptively simple ceramics. Aside from the wares produced by the imperial kilns, Huizong's favorites also drank tea from simple black Jian ware bowls.[30] This austere stoneware embodied a highly naturalistic aesthetic, making it an appropriate accouterment for literati-style tea connoisseurship.

During Huizong's reign, courtiers also embraced the competitive drinking games that had started in Fujian.[31] Although located far from the capital, Fujian had earned recognition as the heartland of fine tea, so tea buffs in the emperor's circle took careful note of drinking customs there. Moreover, regular postings of bureaucrats to oversee Fujian tea fields gave the officialdom firsthand experience with this distant cultural aesthetic. Huizong eagerly embraced Fujian-style whipped tea and patronized palace contests to see who could prepare tea with the finest foam. Injecting a competitive element into tea drinking not only made it more fun, but also opened up opportunities for talented individuals to distinguish themselves from the crowd. In this respect, whipped tea differed enormously from the stiff ceremonial of early Tang court tea rituals. In emphasizing personal accomplishment, Huizong abandoned conformity as a cultural ideal. Instead he focused on the individual cultivation, providing talented tea men with an opportunity to excel before their peers. While tea might seem like a frivolous pursuit on the surface, changing practices in the tea world embodied a profound cultural shift toward a spirit of humanism celebrating the individual.

NOTES

1. Andreas Anter, *Max Weber's Theory of the Modern State: Origins, Structure and Significance*, trans. Keith Tribe (Houndmills, UK: Palgrave Macmillan, 2014), 29–35.
2. Benjamin I. Schwartz, *The World of Thought in Ancient China* (Cambridge, MA: The Belknap Press of Harvard University Press, 1985), 67.
3. Fang Jian, "Tang Song chali chasu shulue," *Minsu yanjiu* 4 (1998): 74–75; Zhu Nailiang, "Tangdai cha wenhua yu Lu Yu 'Cha jing,'" *Nongye kaogu* 2 (1995): 59.
4. Marcel Mauss, *The Gift: The Form and Reason for Exchange in Archaic Societies*, trans. W. D. Halls (New York: W.W. Norton & Co., 2000).
5. Shen Songqin, "Liang Song yincha fengsu yu chaci," *Zhejiang Daxue xuebao* 31, no. 1 (2001): 70–76.
6. Wang Yongping, "Tangdai gongting yincha," *Yinshi wenhua yanjiu* 13, no. 1 (2005): 100; Gong Zhi, *Zhongguo gongcha* (Hangzhou: Zhejiang sheying, 2003), 33.
7. Gong, *Zhongguo gongcha*, 30.
8. Zhou Mi, *Wulin jiushi*, in *Jingyin Wenyuange Siku quanshu*, ed. Ji Yun et al. (Taipei: Taiwan shangwu, 1983), v. 590, p. 264 (8:3a).
9. For a description of this system and the carefully calibrated strategy behind it see Jia Lifang, "Jianxi Mingchao zhi Zang de junshi sixiang," *Xizang Minzu Xueyuan xuebao* 32, no. 2 (2011): 31–33, 66.
10. Gong, *Zhongguo gongcha*, 28.
11. Bret Hinsch, "Textiles and Female Virtue in Early Imperial Chinese Historical Writing," *Nan Nü* 5, no. 2 (2003): 191–96.
12. Wang Xinying, "Tangdai tugong zhidu tanxi," *Tianzhong xuekan* 27, no. 5 (2012): 90–93.

13. Tong Qiqing, "Tang Song shiqi Zhejiang cha wenhua de fazhan," *Nongye kaogu* 4 (1997): 27.

14. Wang Lin and Zhang Wei, "Tang zisun gongcha yanjiu," *Anhui wenxue* 9 (2010): 143–44.

15. Lü Weixin, "Tangdai gongcha zhidu de xingcheng he fazhan," *Chaye tongbao* 1 (1995): 257–88.

16. Cai Quanbao, "Chuan Qin Huzhou zisun lai—Tangdai de gongcha yu gongshui," *Nongye kaogu* 2 (1995): 266–67.

17. Zhu Zhongsheng, *Bei Song cha zhi shengchan yu jingji* (Taipei: Taiwan xuesheng, 1985) describes the Song tribute tea bureaucracy in great detail.

18. Shi Shaohua, *Songdai yong chashi yanjiu* (Taipei: Wenjin, 1996), 52.

19. Shen Gua, *Benchao chafa*, in *Zhongguo gudai chaye quanshu*, ed. Ruan Haogeng et al. (Hangzhou: Zhejiang sheying, 1999), 84–88.

20. Gong, *Zhongguo gongcha*, 6–12. Fan Jingduo, "Tang Song shidai de chabing" *Nongye kaogu* 4 (1995): 184–86 describes the major types of Tang and Song dynasty tea disks.

21. Shen Dongmei, "Lun Songdai Beiyuan guanbei gongcha," *Zhejiang shehui kexue* 7 (1997): 98. For a history of the Beiyuan tea fields see Zheng Lisheng, "Beiyuan chashi," *Nongye kaogu* 2 (1991): 203–7. Gong Zhi, "Manhua Songdai Beiyuan gongcha," *Nongye kaogu* 2 (1998): 209–12, and Gong, *Zhongguo gongcha*, 61–80 describe Beiyuan tea during the Song.

22. Yang Xun, "Jian yao tuhao zhan de xingqi yu Songdai gongting doucha wenhua," *Shoudu Shifan Daxue xuebao* 1 (2011): 73.

23. Shi, *Songdai yong chashi yanjiu*, 88–97.

24. Xu Jingmei, "Songdai chashizhong de gongcha caizhi tese," *Dazhong wenyi* 12 (2011): 167.

25. Xiong Fan, *Xuanhe Beiyuan gongcha lu* , in *Qinding siku quanshu* (Taipei: Taiwan shangwu yinshuguan, n.d.), vol. 844, p. 646 (20a) ("Yuyuan caicha ge," poem 4).

26. Nunome Chōhū, *Chūgoku cha no bunkashi* (Tokyo: Kyūbun, 2001), 149–57 describes the Famen tea ware in detail, and compares the objects in this trove to written accounts. Yu Yue, *Chalu licheng: Zhongguo cha wenhua liubian jianshi* (Beijing: Guangming ribao, 1999), 56–59 describes Tang court tea drinking customs.

27. Gong, *Zhongguo gongcha*, 28–30, 34 discusses the relation of various Tang emperors to tea.

28. Yu Wenxia, "Cong 'Daguan chalun' kan Song Huizong de cha wenhua qingjie ji Songren chadao," *Nongye kaogu* 2 (2005): 61.

29. Zhao Ji, *Daguan chalun*, in *Zhongguo gudai chaye quanshu*, ed. Ruan Haogeng et al. (Hangzhou: Zhejiang sheying, 1999), 89.

30. Yang, "Jian yao tuhao zhan de xingqi yu Songdai gongting doucha wenhua," 74.

31. Yu, "Cong 'Daguan chalun' kan Song Huizong de cha wenhua qingjie ji Songren chadao," 62–63.

3

LU YU

One extraordinary person took a mundane beverage and elevated it into one of China's most meaningful cultural icons. By treating tea as a serious subject, the tea connoisseur Lu Yu convinced legions of readers to regard it with respect. His monumental book *The Classic of Tea (Cha jing)* subjected every aspect of tea to detailed analysis, proving it worthy of sustained study and reflection. In presenting tea drinking as an elegant pursuit, Lu imbued it with intellectual and spiritual depth. And in addition to writing the most important book about tea, Lu Yu also built up a network of connections with courtiers, literati, erudite Buddhist monks, and other tastemakers, convincing them to venerate this drink as a token of high culture.

Lu Yu estimated his year of birth as 733, although he admitted that he did not know anything about where he was born or his parents' identity.[1] A compassionate monk named Zhiji, residing at the Longgai Temple in what is now Shaanxi, took pity on this orphan and adopted him. Zhiji used fortune-telling to choose a name for the infant, selecting one from a random passage in the *Classic of Changes (Yi jing)*.[2] Fortunately for Lu Yu, he had come under the care of an able guardian who saw that he had a good education. The Tang dynasty witnessed the flourishing of Buddhist culture in China, and many monasteries served as important centers of scholarship and culture. Lu benefitted from growing up in this stimulating atmosphere. Moreover, Buddhist monks pioneered tea culture and initiated the promotion of tea drinking into a lofty pursuit, providing Lu with the nucleus of his influential vision of tea.

Zhiji raised this orphan boy expecting that he would eventually follow in his guardian's footsteps and become a monk as well. At age nine Lu commenced an intensive study of the Buddhist canon in preparation for eventually taking the tonsure, with the assumption that he would spend the rest of his life as a cleric. However, Lu showed little interest in religious texts, nor did the prospect of permanent confinement within temple walls appeal to him. Instead of memorizing Buddhist sutras, this bookish boy preferred to read the Confucian classics and other secular works.

Eventually Lu Yu declared that he would never become a monk. Zhiji did not take the news well and punished the boy for his waywardness by forcing him to do the most unpleasant menial jobs at the temple, including construction work, cleaning toilets, and herding animals. Despite these hardships, Lu persevered in his secular studies. Deprived of paper, he used sticks of bamboo and even the sides of cattle as his copybook. Finally an educated gentleman took pity on this clever orphan and loaned him a book of poetry. When Zhiji saw Lu Yu squatting near the cattle excitedly chanting poems, he finally recognized his ward's determination and talent. From that time forward, he supported Lu's decision to pursue a secular education.

In imperial China, acquiring an education involved considerable hardship, as teachers often subjected their students to frequent beatings and other punishments. Nevertheless, Lu Yu put up with these privations and excelled in his studies. The style and contents of *The Classic of Tea* testify to his educational attainments. Lu wrote clearly and fluently, displaying easy familiarity with pertinent historical and literary knowledge. A classical education also allowed Lu Yu to enter literati and court circles as a peer. Once he found himself in the company of educated gentlemen, he could promote his ideas about tea in a cultured manner that his audience found convincing.

In addition to academic studies, Lu Yu's introduction to the art of tea also began in his youth. The monks in his monastery regularly drank this beverage, so he grew up around tea utensils. Although most people of the time did not consider tea very important, Lu found this pursuit intriguing and showed an unusual talent for preparing the beverage, earning Zhiji's praise for his skill. Lu Yu eventually completed a com-

Figure 3.1. Lu Yu

prehensive secular education while also becoming familiar with Buddhist wisdom. This refined young man cut an impressive figure, attracting the notice of influential gentlemen who appreciated his learning and good taste.

In 755 the Rebellion of An Lushan commenced, throwing China into chaos. Civil war upended normal life for the next eight years as loyalist and rebel armies made northern China their battlefield. In search of safe haven, Lu Yu fled the monastery where he had grown up and headed south along with millions of other refugees. Although this involuntary exile involved considerable privation, it also broadened his horizons. Lu had already made some useful connections and used them to gain introductions to educated gentlemen and monks in south China, where he continued his studies. This unexpected contact with southern culture had an important impact on his views of tea. Discriminating gentlemen in the south had begun pushing at the aesthetic margins, lending their regional culture a sense of exciting dynamism. Lu Yu's forced wanderings exposed him to southern ideas of elegance, which further refined his taste and stimulated him to reassess his preconceptions of high culture. In 758 he studied tea at the Qixia temple in the southern metropolis of Jinling, known today as Nanjing, an experience that seems to have had a major impact on his own ideas about the subject. Finally in 760 he settled in Huzhou, officially concluding his studies.

After learning so much, Lu finally felt ready to create something new. While living in Huzhou he became an active poet and participated in literary circles with other educated gentlemen. Besides exchanging poems with other writers, Lu also wrote linked verses in cooperation with forty-eight poets, attesting to his acceptance into the local poetry scene.[3] He published his works together with those of his bookish companions, earning him recognition as an honored member of the literary elite. Lu enjoyed a reputation for polymath erudition. Besides his skill at poetry and calligraphy, he also wrote knowledgeably about history, geography, and various other subjects.

Although Lu Yu had many literary friends, the time he spent together with a cultured monk named Jiaoran exerted a profound influence on his ideas about tea. Jiaoran enjoyed a reputation as a major cultural figure who achieved a degree of fame in his own lifetime, and he is still remembered today as a talented poet. This educated monk seems to have felt extremely comfortable around a talented young literatus who had grown up in a Buddhist setting. The pair often met to drink tea and write poetry together, forming a fast friendship based on their shared interests. Some of Jiaoran's poems even mention Lu Yu by name, attesting to the depth of their connection.[4] Of course these poems also describe the pleasures of their tea drinking sessions, showing that at this point in his life Lu Yu indeed drank tea frequently and enthusiastically. When it came to tea, Lu was no poseur.

Jiaoran's poems portray Lu Yu as a Daoist-style recluse, living in a country cottage bounded by chrysanthemums in the style of the famed poetic hermit Tao Qian. Framing his friend within the imagery of Daoist reclusion shows that Lu considered tea to be one part of a comprehensive lifestyle dedicated to the pursuit of the rigorous aesthetic and spiritual cultivation. This imagery also accounts for Lu's rejection of luxurious tea drinking customs. The empty-headed extravagance of courtly tea had no place within this deliberately humble Daoist worldview.

During these pleasant days devoted to poetry, tea, and cultured conversation with like-minded friends, Lu Yu composed his famous *The Classic of Tea*. It seems that he began to write this book before 761 and continued to edit it over the years. He probably did not officially release the final version until 780. Despite the difficulty of disseminating a book in an age before mass printing, this work nevertheless enjoyed an enthusiastic reception. Lu Yu immediately attained a reputation as the leading expert on the subject, and prominent gentlemen began to seek him out to solicit his advice about tea connoisseurship.

During the Tang, as in other eras of imperial history, the typical man of letters dreamed of one day serving as a government official, as a post in the bureaucracy promised both tangible remuneration and prestige. In spite of his humble background, Lu Yu's varied accomplishments had earned him the respect of the powerful, and so influential patrons arranged a job for him. In 777 Lu bid farewell to his friends in Huzhou and traveled to take up a government post, serving in a succession of bureaucratic positions. During his time in office he even had an audience with Emperor Tang Taizong, an enthusiastic tea lover determined to elevate the tone of court drinking rituals. Impressed by Lu Yu's reputation in this field, Taizong ordered him to teach his courtiers the proper way to make tea. This experience brought Lu's forward-looking views on tea to the attention of the most powerful and influential people in China, bestowing an aura of authority upon him that helps account for the enormous impact of his ideas.

Despite the demands of his official duties, Lu nevertheless also found time not only to drink tea but also to continue dabbling in literature. He remained an active presence in the world of poetry. Lu considered tea inseparable from literature, a view that sums up the importance he accorded this beverage. Finally in 793 he retired from office. Although he had grown up in the north, he had come to love southern China and returned there to spend his final years. After retirement he lived quietly until his death in the winter of 804.

Although Lu Yu attained renown as a tea expert in his own lifetime, his posthumous reputation rose to the pinnacle of fame and respect. To subsequent generations, his canny insights into tea made him seem almost divine. Henceforth, whenever someone mentioned "the god of tea" (*chashen*), this could only mean Lu Yu. For example, a Ming dynasty poem by Tong Hanchen describes a reverie brought on by tasting Longjing tea so sublime that the poet finds himself face-to-face with the resurrected spirit of Lu Yu, who has assumed the form of a god.[5] Poets frequently invoked Lu's name in many different contexts as a backhanded synonym for tea drinking. Sad poems of parting, nostalgic poems of remembrance, and enthusiastic elegies all mention Lu Yu by name. For centuries tea drinkers continued to write poems of mourning for this beloved tea expert, lamenting his passing long after his death.[6]

Generations of readers continued to show their enthusiastic appreciation for *The Classic of Tea*, so publishers found it a sure way to make money. Editions regularly appeared through the Song, Ming, and Qing dynasties, often with a new preface attesting yet again to this work's value and incomparable stature. Lu Yu's work on tea also served as a model that inspired numerous essays and books about every aspect of the subject during subsequent eras.

So why was Lu Yu so important? He certainly cannot be credited with popularizing tea drinking. Before he wrote *The Classic of Tea*, this beverage had already become ubiquitous at all levels of society. Nor can he be considered the first to see tea as a prestigious item for use on special occasions. Rituals and celebrations at court already featured tea, which the emperor and high officials enjoyed with splendid vessels delicately wrought from gold and silver, drinking it with elaborate ceremony. Sacrifices to gods and ancestors already included tea. Dowries included tea. Tea had become a standard gift of state to important allies. And cultured monks and poets regularly drank tea.

Lu Yu did not invent tea drinking or bring it to the attention of the elite. Instead he owed his prominence to the simple fact that he was the first person to write a book dedicated to the insight that tea could be a cultured pursuit. Because this drink had already become so commonplace, the stage had already been set for a breakthrough in connoisseurship.[7] Although tea had become a standard theme in poetry and authors mentioned it in passing in their prose works, up to this point no one had written a specialized book on the subject. Lu realized that this unique beverage deserved careful study, and in *The Classic of Tea* he subjects every feature to detailed treatment. This book has endured not just because of its comprehensive scope, covering virtually every aspect of the topic, but also due to Lu's clear and elegant style. Most importantly, he presented an eloquent manifesto for his belief that tea drinking should be considered a form of high culture.

The Classic of Tea covers history, production, brewing, medicinal properties, and appreciation, providing the reader with a far-reaching overview of tea. Lu did not limit himself to dry facts or the technical side of tea preparation, but reflected on the subjective psychological aspects of connoisseurship as well. Most importantly, Lu Yu implicitly rejected the luxurious excesses of courtly tea drinking, turning his back on the vacuous obsession with costly tea implements. Instead he advocated a subtle style of connoisseurship, emphasizing subjective factors such as a correct psychological state, aesthetic cultivation, and good taste.

Although concise, this little book nevertheless aims at achieving an encyclopedic scope. Lu Yu begins not with grand philosophical musings, but rather by commenting on the medicinal uses of this beverage. This subdued beginning reflects the primal origins of tea as a medicinal tonic, a view still common during the Tang dynasty and indeed widely held today. He also provides the reader with a brief history of the drink, charting its rise to prominence.

Much of the book consists of a detailed discussion of the various vessels and implements needed to store, brew, and drink tea. As tea leaves still came in compressed blocks and had to be ground down to a powder, during the Tang dynasty proper preparation required an elab-

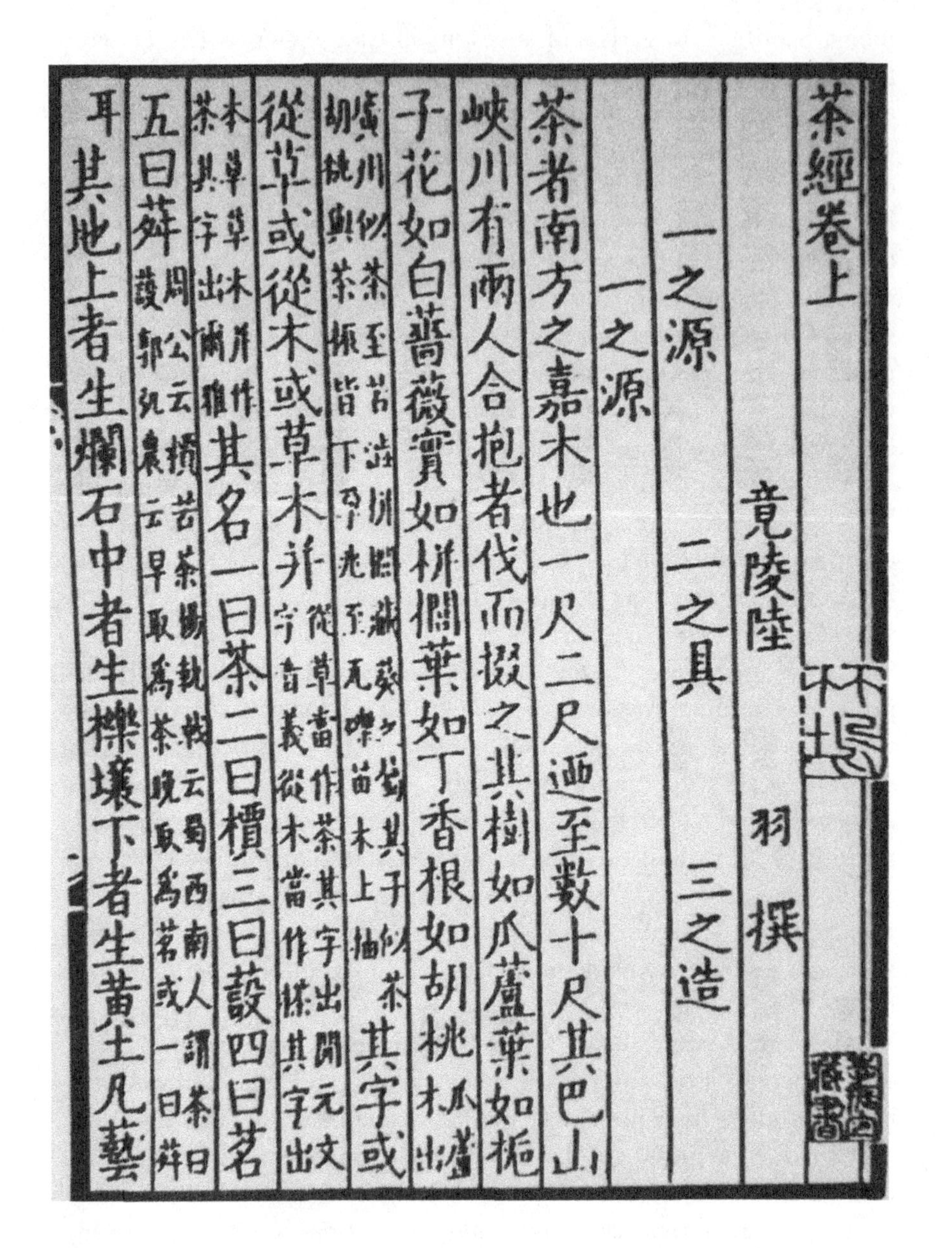

茶經卷上

竟陵陸羽撰

一之源 二之具 三之造

一之源

茶者南方之嘉木也一尺二尺迺至數十尺其巴山峽川有兩人合抱者伐而掇之其樹如瓜蘆葉如梔子花如白薔薇實如栟櫚葉如丁香根如胡桃瓜蘆木出廣州似茶至苦澀栟櫚蒲葵之屬其子似茶胡桃與茶根皆下孕兆至瓦礫苗木上抽其字或從草或從木或草木并從草當作茶其字出開元文字音義從木當作梌其字出本草草木并作荼其字出爾雅其名一曰茶二曰檟三曰蔎四曰茗五曰荈周公云檟苦荼楊執戟云蜀西南人謂茶曰蔎郭弘農云早取為茶晚取為茗或一曰荈耳其地上者生爛石中者生櫟壤下者生黃土凡藝

Figure 3.2. ***The Classic of Tea***

orate set of paraphernalia. Anyone planning to brew tea would need to understand the identity of each item of this daunting battery of utensils, determine which were best, and know how to use them correctly. Today we brew tea very differently, so modern readers will not find this lengthy section very germane. At the time, however, Lu Yu's clear explanations of these technical matters provided drinkers with an invaluable guide to a complicated subject. According to Lu, preparing tea in a formal situation requires twenty-four implements. He declares that if the drinker lacks even one of these items, it would be better to skip making tea altogether rather than proceed with the wrong equipage.[8] Although Lu became famous for advancing the philosophical and spiritual aspects of tea culture, he nevertheless comes across as a stickler for the proper mechanics of tea making. Even so, he had a good reason for obsessing over technique. Lu firmly believed that the serious drinker must master the routine mechanical aspects of brewing tea before going on to explore its transcendent side.

Archaeological finds have recently confirmed the accuracy of Lu Yu's careful descriptions of tea wares. Scholars examining the luxurious implements uncovered at the Famen Temple have confirmed that he provided an extremely accurate account of contemporary tea ware. So Lu did not present the reader with an idealized view of tea but instead described tea preparation as members of the elite actually practiced it at the time. Although he did not intend to alter the basics of how tea was made, later in the book he emphasizes the spirit of naturalism conducive to tea appreciation, goading drinkers to abandon showy luxury for a far more modest, casual, introspective, and confident style of drinking. Although the basic mechanics of preparation may have been the same as before, the mindset differed considerably. Lu transformed tea culture by turning inward and advocating an innovative new spirit of profound simplicity.

In some respects Lu Yu's views place him at a crossroads between the previous emphasis on luxury and the subsequent literati quest for refinement and elegance. For example, he recommends silver as the best material for the cauldron that holds the hot tea water. Even though silver might seem like an extravagant material that might distract from the pursuit of deeper spiritual concerns, he justifies this choice by contending that this precious material is best for keeping water pure.[9] When we realize that the most likely substitute for silver would have been iron, his pronouncement seems reasonable, as iron might impart a metallic taste to tea water. Even so, his endorsement of silver tea implements still betrays the residual influence of an earlier tea aesthetic that prized costly luxury. Song dynasty tea men would have considered flashy silver tea ware embarrassingly vulgar.

In other respects, however, Lu Yu's taste foreshadows the emerging literati style of tea. For example, he proudly describes the metal brazier he uses to boil tea water, admiring not only its attractive appearance but also the inscriptions in ancient script written on three legs.[10] Lu believed that these archaic characters enhanced the nobility of the piece. He valued this brazier not just due to its functionality or even beauty, but also because connections with history and literature elevated it into an artifact of high culture. This desire to unify tea with other aspects of literati taste prefigures the emergence of a new and far more refined culture of tea.

Next Lu describes at great length the correct method for preparing tea. First a block of compressed leaves has to be toasted over a fire or steamed to purify the taste. Then one cuts off the right sized chunk of leaves and slowly grinds it down to a fine powder in a mortar. Lu does not consider this an easy matter, and warns that the tea could easily be ruined at this stage. The serious drinker has to use only the best possible water, pure and tasty. Many places lack appropriate water, so it might be difficult to acquire. Lu discusses the different kinds of water and the qualities of each in regard to making tea.[11] Having procured proper water, the drinker heats it to the proper degree, judging the temperature by sight. As Tang drinkers still added salt to their tea, he notes that the liquid has to be salted to the right strength prior to ladling it into bowls. The drinker then spoons the correct amount of tea powder into the bowl and whips it vigorously with a whisk, mixing it into the water to create an even infusion with a foamy head. Because observers would judge the tea largely by these bubbles, Lu describes at length the right sort of froth and how to achieve it.[12]

Today's readers will likely come away intimidated by the complexity of this protracted process. However, to the Tang connoisseur, these difficulties presented opportunities as well as challenges. Whoever mastered this intricate procedure and made tea with grace and confidence could win a reputation as a true tea man (*charen*). If making tea involved only dipping a tea bag into a mug of tepid water, there would not be any room for individual expression or the pursuit of excellence. But by deliberately complicating every aspect of the process in the name of aesthetics and taste, Lu Yu provided openings for culturally ambitious gentlemen to show off their skill. The deliberate introduction of arcana into tea drinking, such as the intimidating array of tea implements and detailed classifications of water, also gave the tea buff a chance to master complicated details and then show off esoteric knowledge to impressed onlookers.

Complicating tea drinking turned it into a kind of performance art that the tea expert could use as a medium for displaying his exquisite taste. For example, Lu Yu explains in detail how the color of a ceramic bowl affects the color of tea, warning that a drinker should never use a vessel that gives the liquid an unpleasant tint.[13] Aestheticizing this sort of minutia took tea connoisseurship to new heights, giving those with proper sensitivity to these sorts of matters regular occasions to showcase their refinement and expertise, thereby staking a claim to privileged status.

Initially readers valued *The Classic of Tea* largely because it provides clear and authoritative instructions on the practical techniques of tea preparation, clearly a complicated procedure at the time. The method for brewing tea has changed so much over the centuries that most of this information has since become useless to drinkers today. Even so, people continued to read and value this book. In fact, Lu Yu's reputation continued to rise even as his instructions on how to make tea became increasingly obsolete. His inspiring spirit of connoisseurship explains this apparent contradiction. For many readers, Lu's meticulous attention to detail motivated them to deepen their own appreciation. Although they may have prepared tea very differently from Tang drinkers, generations of drinkers have nevertheless continued to follow in Lu's footsteps by subjecting every aspect of tea to the same combination of technical rigor and aesthetic sensitivity.

Lu Yu believed that these procedural details constitute the inescapable grounding for higher forms of connoisseurship. He notes that although drinkers will invariably assess the quality of a bowl of tea, their judgments have varying worth.[14] Because most people have not mastered the practical aspects of preparation and do not understand the characteristics of each kind of tea, they can easily err in their judgments. Mastering this complex body of technical information lends one's opinions far greater weight. When the drinker not only knows how to brew superb tea but can also appreciate it with discernment, it becomes a rich experience that engages the mind and all of the senses.

Lu coins a metaphor to justify his connoisseurship. He notes that when people live in a house, they make an effort to decorate it. When they buy clothes, they try to choose something attractive. Likewise, when they drink tea, they should want to refine the experience. In other words, Lu considers the aestheticization of tea an extension of the natural human desire to beautify life. He lists nine factors that influence the quality of tea: manufacture, selection, implements, fire, water, roasting, grinding, brewing, and drinking.[15] As each one of these steps can be endlessly tweaked and improved, making and enjoying tea provides ample openings for the exercise of connoisseurship. When the drinker gains full control over each stage of this process, a bowl of tea can inspire delight. The successful connoisseur turns a humble beverage into a thing of beauty and even profundity.

The wildly enthusiastic reception of *The Classic of Tea* attests to the profound shift in the mentality of literati during the Tang and Song dynasties. During this era, educated gentlemen experienced an awakening of individual consciousness. When Lu Yu wrote this book, the terrible chaos of the An Lushan Rebellion had shattered many people's faith in conventional ethics and ideas. Instead of simply accepting and imitating time-tested examples of orthodox thought, art, and behavior, skeptics began to view the world from a more personal and idiosyncratic perspective. This expanding psychological space allowed Lu Yu the freedom to conceptualize tea differently, presenting it to his readers as a beautiful and profound cultural medium worthy of sustained contemplation. Intelligent drinkers quickly realized that drinking tea in a cultured style offered them novel opportunities to express their own accomplishments, cultivation, ideas, and emotions. Lu Yu taught his readers how to use tea to show the world aspects of themselves that had previously remained hidden. As drinkers followed his advice, tea culture unleashed individualistic expression.

Besides issuing a call for connoisseurship, Lu Yu also discussed the potential profundity of the drinking experience, imbuing tea with even greater significance. Most drinkers had previously focused on outward niceties such as procuring the most luxurious implements. In contrast, Lu Yu transformed tea culture by guiding the drinker inward. *The Classic of Tea* argues that this beverage can become a lofty cultural pursuit, a source of personal cultivation, and even a platform for spiritual attainment.

Lu takes tea drinking beyond even the bounds of connoisseurship to imbue it with even greater depth. For example, the opening lines of *The Classic of Tea* assert that the way of tea encompasses frugality and virtue (*jiande*). At first glance, the first term of this pair seems to declare Lu's rejection of gaudy luxury. But in fact, he is echoing the ideal of frugal simplicity (*jianpu*) central to Chan (Zen) Buddhism.[16] This passage begs a key question: *why* did Lu object to the pursuit of luxury as a method for enjoying tea? Given his sensitivity to connoisseurship, it might seem that he considered the common obsession with cost to be hopelessly vulgar. However, this passage takes his view of the matter even further. Lu sees the pursuit of modest simplicity as a kind of spiritual ideal. By casting off our obsession with flashy externals, we can begin to perceive tea as a tool for personal cultivation. Frugality sweeps

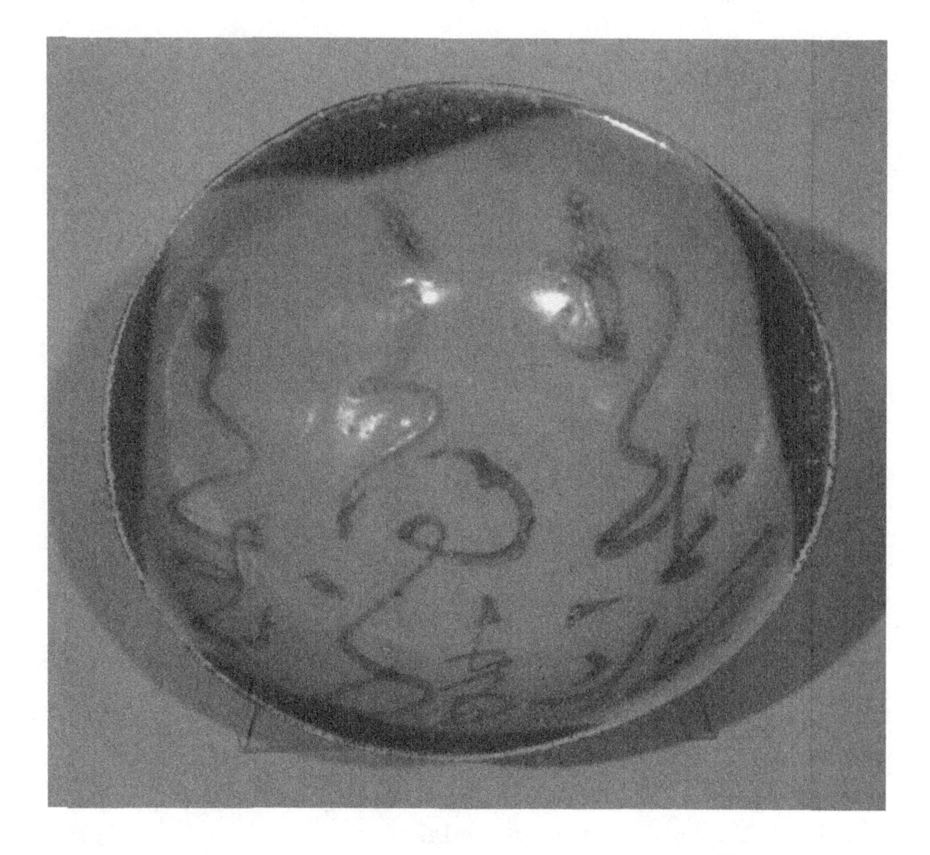

Figure 3.3. A humble bowl

away the nonessential, thus allowing the drinker to contemplate the most important things in life while holding tea bowl in hand.

Although Lu Yu had a Buddhist upbringing, and his interaction with cultured monks led him to link tea to Zen-style modesty, his view of tea resonates most closely with Daoism.[17] He believed that tea could nurture a Daoist mindset, bringing the drinker closer to nature, inviting quiet contemplation, and providing an escape from daily cares. By imbuing tea with spiritual significance, Lu Yu transformed the standard view of one of the most common items in daily life. Drinkers began to pay far more attention to the bowl in front of them. Although tea had once been no more than a pleasant beverage, perceptive readers began to wake up to tea's intellectual and spiritual potential. As the latent possibilities unfolded, drinkers raised their own lives to a higher standard of cultivation while grasping the beauty and profundity that can be gained from taking tea as a serious cultured pursuit.

NOTES

1. For a concise biography of Lu Yu see Lu Yu and Shen Dongmei, *Cha jing jiaozhu* (Taipei: Yuhe wenhua, 2009), 3–9; James A. Benn, *Tea in China: A Religious and Cultural History* (Honolulu: University of Hawaii Press, 2015), 96–111. For a more detailed discussion of Lu Yu's life and works see Shu Yujie, *Zhongguo cha wenhua jingo daguan* (Beijing: Dianzi gongye, 1999), 381–484.
2. During the Tang dynasty, poets referred to Lu Yu by many other names as well. Liu Jing, "Tangren yong Lu Yu shi yanjiu: cha he Lu Yu de shenghuo, 'Cha jing' de xiezuo ji qi rensheng chutan," *Nongye kaogu* 2 (2011): 132.
3. Liu Jing, "Tangren yong Lu Yu shi yanjiu: cha he Lu Yu de shenghuo, 'Cha jing' de xiezuo ji qi rensheng chutan," *Nongye kaogu* 2 (2011): 136.
4. Feng Fade, "Tianxia mingshan seng zhan bian, conglai senglü duo ai cha—luelun Tangdai Jiao Ran zhuseng chashi," *Nongye kaogu* 2 (1995): 192–93.
5. Liao Jianzhi, *Mingdai cha wenhua yishu* (Taipei: Xiuwei, 2007), 211.
6. Liu, "Tangren yong Lu Yu shi yanjiu: cha he Lu Yu de shenghuo, 135–36.
7. Zhu Nailiang, "Tangdai cha wenhua yu Lu Yu 'Cha jing,'" *Nongye kaogu* 2 (1995): 58.
8. Lu, *The Classic of Tea,* trans. Francis Ross Carpenter (Hopewell, NJ: Ecco, 1974), 151; Lu, *Cha jing jiaozhu*, 9:182.
9. Lu, *The Classic of Tea,* 82; Lu, *Cha jing jiaozhu*, 4: 72.

10. Lu, *The Classic of Tea,* 77; Lu, *Cha jing jiaozhu*, 4:70–71.

11. Discussions of good water began long before the Tang. E. N. Anderson, *Food and Environment in Early and Medieval China* (Philadelphia: University of Pennsylvania Press, 2014), 86.

12. Lu, *The Classic of Tea,* 103–11; Lu, *Cha jing jiaozhu*, 5:92–93.

13. Lu, *The Classic of Tea,* 92–93; Lu, *Cha jing jiaozhu*, 4:74.

14. Lu, *The Classic of Tea*, 74; Lu, *Cha jing jiaozhu*, 3:61.

15. Lu, *The Classic of Tea,* 117–18; Lu, *Cha jing jiaozhu*, 6:99.

16. Lu Jianwei, "Lu Yu sixiangzhong de chanxing yixiang," *Huzhou Shizhuan xuebao* 2 (1996): 54.

17. Lai Gongou, *Cha zhe rui zhi: Zhongguo cha wenhua yu ru shi dao* (Beijing: Guangming ribao, 1999), 8.

4

CONNOISSEURSHIP

Lu Yu inspired talented and tasteful gentlemen across China to take tea very seriously. As increasing number of readers pondered *The Classic of Tea*, the idea that this particular beverage ranks as something very special, laden with profound significance and aesthetic possibility, became a standard assumption. Over the following centuries, cultured gentlemen wrote numerous books discussing every aspect of tea. Some authors followed in the footsteps of Lu Yu and composed general works on the subject. Others catalogued the numerous varieties of tea, even writing books on obscure regional specialties. They often critiqued various teas in detail and ranked them according to quality. And because Lu Yu had established premium water as essential for good tea, connoisseurs analyzed that topic as well, recording the qualities of water from famous streams and springs and grading them according to their suitability for making tea. Other books explored highly technical aspects of proper brewing or the multitude of tea wares. Some tea buffs collected anecdotes and miscellaneous facts about tea. Taken together, this outpouring of highly informed writing attests to the sophistication of tea connoisseurship.

Many of these books have since been lost, including some that experts once held in high regard.[1] The titles of these vanished books suggest that late Tang and Song drinkers had access to an impressive body of writing on the subject. Some lost works seem to have been quite important and exerted a significant impact on tea culture. For example, a book that ranked different types of water, considered a

Figure 4.1. Cai Xiang

standard statement on the subject at the time, has since disappeared.[2] Because so few people participated in the loftiest circles of connoisseurship, tea books inevitably had very limited circulation, so a work could easily be lost forever if the few existent copies happened to fall into the wrong hands. Some tea men realized to their horror that treasured works might easily be consigned to oblivion. To guarantee the survival of at least one major book, *Records of Tea* (*Cha lu*) by Cai Xiang (1012–1067) was engraved on stone in 1064 so that rubbings could be made and distributed across China.[3] This strategy worked, and Cai's work remains an enduring statement on many aspects of tea culture.

Although some masterpieces from the formative age of tea culture have been lost, many others survived, including most of the main works. As time passed, the rise of print culture ensured wider circulation, so fewer tea books succumbed to the vicissitudes of time. Most of the major works from the Ming and Qing have been handed down intact.[4] Taken together, this rich body of writing documents in detail how tea connoisseurship developed over the centuries.

Following Lu Yu's example, tea experts began to look carefully at growing and processing. They realized that no matter how meticulously the drinker prepares a bowl of tea, only properly processed leaves can yield a satisfying beverage. By the Song dynasty, production had been brought under control and refined to produce a superb product. Emperor Song Huizong could declare with confidence, "From olden times to the present, skill at harvesting, work at processing, competence at grading, and excellence at brewing have all reached an apex."[5]

The rising quality and reputation of tea led drinkers to take it much more seriously. Lu Yu's friend Jiaoran seems to have been the one who coined the term "way of tea" (*chadao*).[6] As a monk, Jiaoran had become accustomed to viewing the world through the lens of religion, making him acutely sensitive to the latent profundity of tea culture. By calling tea a "way" (*dao*), a standard term in religious and philosophical discourse, Jiaoran evoked abundant associations that would have immediately resonated with his audience. This word implies a set of standard rules, such that the Japanese appropriation of these characters is usually translated "tea ceremony." However, calling tea drinking a "way" also suggests that it can be morally and spiritually uplifting. Jiaoran's insight that tea could be a *dao* inspired drinkers to study and refine every aspect of this increasingly profound pursuit.

Increasing attention to technical details, such as information regarding proper tea farming, shows the impact of the connoisseur mentality on discussions of tea. Although Emperor Song Huizong obviously had no personal experience working in a tea field, he nevertheless wrote about the particulars of tea farming in surprising detail. His interest in the commonplace beginnings of the tea he drank, tracing it all the way back to mountain fields in distant Fujian, attests to the rigor of Song connoisseurship. Drinkers took a keen interest in the specifics of growing and harvesting, realizing that every aspect of production had to be refined if tea were to reach its ultimate potential. In his insightful book, Huizong starts from the basics and emphasizes a keen sensitivity to terroir as essential to producing great tea. The amount of sunlight, quality of soil, and terrain all affect the kind of leaves that a particular patch of land will yield. The tea tree also requires the right weather. And of course the leaves must be picked at the proper time to ensure optimal quality. Huizong sums up the matter succinctly in observing, "When yin and yang are both adequate, the taste of tea is suitable."[7]

After being harvested and then steamed and dried to perfection, the compressed leaves inevitably underwent a period of transport and storage prior to consumption. As tea sat dormant, it might absorb unwanted moisture that could negatively affect the flavor of the final drink. Experts discussed possible solutions to this problem, advising readers on the precise method for toasting a tea disk to drive out any excess moisture without degrading it.[8] If tea had been in storage for some time, it might even be necessary to heat it to body temperature for three days in order to gently evaporate all of the accumulated dampness. Most importantly, the flame could not be too intense lest the leaves be ruined by an acrid burnt flavor. When a tea disk had been covered with a protective oily coating, the initial preparations became even more involved. The disk had to be soaked briefly in hot water to soften the oily coating, which was then scraped off. Lightly toasting the exposed leaves dried them out before they were ground down to a powder.

As connoisseurship evolved, tea aficionados sought to meticulously control every aspect of the preparation and drinking process. Tang and Song authorities discussed each of these factors, both objective and subjective, in minute detail. For example, the famed literatus Ouyang Xiu (1007–1072) described what he considered four essential requirements for the ideal tea drinking experience: fresh leaves, sweet spring water, clean vessels, and fine weather.[9] As these factors became standardized and well understood, enthusiastic drinkers eventually began to construct specialized teahouses (*chaliao*) where every aspect of the environment could be made perfectly suitable for brewing and appreciating tea.[10] Gentlemen usually constructed a teahouse close to their study. This prestigious location physically associated tea drinking with learning, high culture, and the pursuit of self-cultivation. In fact, the term house or hut (*liao*), which describes a humble dwelling, was often used to refer to a monk's quarters. Appropriating this term for a specialized tea drinking venue implied that the drinker intended to undertake a similarly serious spiritual quest.

When perusing old tea books, modern readers will probably be most surprised by the attention that connoisseurs lavished on water. As soon as a self-conscious culture of tea connoisseurship began to emerge during the Tang, Lu Yu stressed the right sort of water as a critical component to good tea. Subsequent writers followed his lead and fleshed out these observations, producing a sophisticated body of writing about the qualities and flavor of water. Many features of good water seem commonsensical. For example, it should not be murky or have a strong taste. However, as with tea, water appreciation encompassed subjective elements as well. For example, when two Tang experts ranked tea water sources in order of quality, they came up with two very different lists. One considered water from the Yangtze River at Nanling the finest, while the other put it at number seven.[11] These discrepancies reveal an ongoing debate among connoisseurs that not only provided them with something to talk about while they waited for the kettle to heat up, but also spurred them to think very deeply about the constituent aspects of the perfect bowl of tea.

Heating the water prior to steeping the leaves required a degree of skill. When preparing fine tea, then as now, one must heat the water to a precise temperature, because excessively hot water brings out unpleasant flavors and odors in some teas. However, without a thermometer, drinkers had no choice but to learn how to recognize the temperature of water based on its appearance. As water becomes hot, scattered bubbles that look like fish eyes begin to appear. At a slightly higher temperature, the bubbles begin to look like strings of pearls. And at a full boil, waves roil the water and it emits steam.[12] Connoisseurship required far more than just being able to talk about the difference between good and bad tea. The tea expert also had to master these sorts of practical details to be able to brew it properly.

When educated gentlemen began to regard tea drinking as a kind of aestheticized performance, they looked at ceramics differently than before. Connoisseurs demanded new kinds of tea ware. In addition to functionality, they believed that bowls and ewers ought to express a mode of beauty compatible with the spirit of tea. So as tea drinking customs shifted, craftsmen had to respond by offering new shapes and glazes. The demands of such discerning consumers inspired potters to unleash their creativity, and in response they came up with inventive new types of tea ware.[13] The rapidly evolving culture of tea heavily influenced the changing styles of Tang and Song ceramics, often guiding shape, color, surface texture, and other characteristics.[14]

Of course the most important aspect of connoisseurship involves appreciating the tea itself. During the Song in particular, detailed criteria emerged for judging color, fragrance, and flavor. Opinionated tea men debated these qualities, using the resulting consensus to judge their tea.[15] Cai Xiang's astute *Records of Tea* captures this atmosphere of perfectionism. A highly educated native of Fujian and one of the greatest calligraphers of the Song dynasty, Cai applied his aesthetic discernment to tea drinking. His book on the subject ranks as the most erudite statement of connoisseurship since Lu Yu's monumental *The Classic of Tea*.

In setting forth the qualities of good tea, Cai covered every aspect of the subject.[16] The discriminating drinker starts by examining the color of the leaves: green, yellow, purple, black, or white. A leaf's color speaks to its type and general quality. The tea disk should also be carefully scrutinized. If it lacks the proper sheen and fragrance, it is probably fake. Once brewed, tea should emit a complex fragrance reminiscent of a heady mix of fruits and herbs. Most importantly, it should impart a natural sweetness. For this reason, the leaves have to be steeped in the right sort of water. Water that lacks inherent sweetness cannot possibly produce sweet tea. Cai goes on and on in this vein for the length of this remarkable book, an eloquent testament to the sophistication of tea connoisseurship during the Song.

The colossal Song literary figure Su Shi (also known as Su Dongpo, 1037–1101) frequently mentioned tea in his poetry, providing another window into the culture of connoisseurship that flourished during his lifetime. For example, drinkers often gave poetic names to tea varieties and disks as a way of evoking an elevated ambiance of literary high culture. Like other tea fans, Su paid close attention to water quality and tea ware. But being a sensitive poet, he also appreciated the subjective side of connoisseurship. Because the environment for tea drinking inevitably influences our perceptions, he believed that it should ideally be consumed outdoors amid natural beauty.[17]

All of this elaborate theorizing about tea might be interesting and potentially useful, but most importantly, a bowl of tea has to taste good. Initially drinkers adulterated their tea with dried fruits and flowers, even adding extremely robust flavors such as camphor and incense. As time went on, however, informed drinkers increasingly preferred to take their tea straight, so the flavor of the leaves came to the foreground of connoisseurship. In his comprehensive *Discussions of Tea in the Daguan Reign Era*, Emperor Song Huizong identifies the main problems that can degrade flavor and make it excessively sour, bitter, or acrid, describing the cause of each kind of flaw. Most often, bad flavor results from using an inferior product or leaves that have been improperly processed.

Huizong points out that tasty tea always exhibits a quality known as *gan*, an insight that became a central tenet of tea connoisseurship.[18] *Gan* refers to the subtle sweetness that resides naturally in certain plants. In contrast to the childish sugary sweetness (*tian*) of candy, only the discerning palate can appreciate the ethereal subtlety of *gan*. While a good tea might exhibit various minor characteristics, it must always be *gan*. The emphasis that Song connoisseurs placed on understated *gan* sweetness helped elevate the way of tea to even greater heights of refinement.

As the varieties of tea proliferated, tasting the many different types, judging their respective quality, and ranking them against one another became an important project for connoisseurs. The poetic oeuvre of Lu You (1125–1209) mentions teas from many places, conveying an impression of the wide variety available on the open market.[19] With the rise of the commercial economy during the Song, merchants transported large quantities of tea from place to place, providing curious drinkers with easy access to exotica from distant regions. Even one appellation could produce extremely varied kinds of tea. For example, the craggy mountains of Jian'an in Fujian shield numerous microclimates, each nurturing a slightly different sort of tea plant.[20] This confusing diversity challenged experts determined to establish a reliable system of classifying and grading each tea.

However much tea connoisseurs might have longed to standardize the reputations for major varieties of tea, the inevitable subjectivity of personal taste rendered impartial judgments impossible. Some drinkers exhibited an independent streak in expressing their disappointment with a famous kind of tea and criticizing it as overrated. In fact, connoisseurs often displayed a healthy skepticism toward orthodox taste, embracing a spirit of individualism when assessing different kinds of tea.[21]

Although opinions varied, Song connoisseurs most often singled out Fujian disks, of the sort used for court tribute tea, as the very finest. In his *Additions to the Classic of Tea (Bu cha jing)*, Zhou Feng declared, "Of the world's teas, those of Jian (Fujian) are the best. And Beiyuan in Jian is the best of those."[22] The renowned connoisseur Cai Xiang concurred, identifying the Fujian "dragon" tea disks prepared for the court as the very finest.[23] However, other types of tea also had their partisans. For example, in the Ming dynasty, expert Yuan Hongdao declared Longjing tea the best and wrote a persuasive essay to prove his assertion.[24]

As connoisseurship developed, the ways of appreciating tea became increasingly abstract. For a tea man to distinguish himself, it was no longer enough to spout off tea arcana while whipping up a good head of foam. Educated drinkers increasingly strove to display their individual sense of taste by ornamenting the way of tea with the trappings of high culture. In particular, they integrated the rich panoply of refined pursuits with tea drinking, bringing this activity into the fold of literati culture. Doing so enhanced the lives of educated gentlemen by providing them with another cultured outlet for expressing their good taste and erudition. Association with literati culture also raised the status of tea, proving it a prestigious pursuit suitable for the genteel.

After the eighth century, literati drinking practices increasingly diverged from those traditionally practiced in Buddhist temples and at court.[25] Late Tang poetry displays a new emphasis on a style of connoisseurship that melded high culture together with the way of tea. *Summarized Records on Ranking Tea (Pincha yaolu)*, published by an enthusiast named Huang Ru around 1075, declared tea an integral part of literati identity and a ubiquitous accompaniment to urbane activities.[26] Major cultural figures such as Su Shi and Ouyang Xiu ardently embraced tea drinking and integrated it into their artistic happenings, mentioning it frequently in their poetry. And educated gentlemen demonstrated an increasing familiarity with tea. For example, poetry began to include technical tea jargon and details regarding growing and processing.

The Song author Li Qingzhao (1081–ca. 1141), one of the most erudite women of her age, captures the increasingly cultured atmosphere of tea drinking with a lively vignette.[27] Although famous tea experts were exclusively male, educated women also participated in tea culture, albeit in a less visible fashion. Because Li grew up in a sophisticated family that nurtured the highest standards of literati culture, she amalgamated tea into her literary games.

> Each time after we finished eating we would return to the study, have a seat, and brew tea. With a pile of books and histories, we would say what event was recorded in which line of which page of which chapter of which volume. Then we would open the books and check to see who won and who lost, thereby determining who drank first and who last. Sometimes when someone was correct we would laugh with delight and lift up our bowls, overturning them so that we could not drink any tea at all.

Tea drinking also served as solace in the face of difficulties. During the Song dynasty, educated officials enjoyed unprecedented power, re-

Figure 4.2. Jun ware bowl

sponsibility, and influence. Although they welcomed their heightened social position, increased responsibilities brought tremendous pressure and anxiety. Moreover, most literati failed to find official employment, despite the new opportunities open to them. In fact, many Song literati found themselves facing the embarrassment of downward mobility. Although educated and cultured, they could not compete with even more intelligent and skilled peers. Too proud to make money from commerce, much less work with their hands, many drifted downward into genteel poverty.

For both successful and failed literati, the highly competitive new social system could be enormously frustrating. As a result, they became acutely aware of the pains and contradictions of human existence, giving them an almost tragic outlook on life.[28] Many turned to tea for consolation after personal setbacks. The culture of transcendence and aestheticism enveloping tea could serve as a refuge from the mundane world of competition.[29] Tea also provided them with an energizing realm of liberated mental space. Whereas numerous rules constricted practical affairs and even many cultured activities, the way of tea stressed naturalism. Encouraged to seek authenticity, educated gentlemen felt relaxed and reinvigorated when they drank tea, becoming more creative as a result. Tea culture thus became an important wellspring of inspiration for writers and artists.

For the ambitious, tea expertise could endow their family with a valuable intangible asset. Even though literati lacked hereditary title, official service nonetheless tended to run in families, which sometimes managed to maintain their high status for generations. Literati identity could gain a degree of stability because it relied on more than just wealth. To be considered a literatus, one had to complete an extensive classical education, participate in (but not necessarily pass) the official examinations, and engage in orthodox cultured pursuits such as poetry, calligraphy, painting, gardening, music—and tea. Fathers could help their sons win acceptance as literati by teaching them these refined activities. Investing time and trouble to become a tea household had practical value for this social group. A tea connoisseur possessed precious knowledge that he could pass down to his progeny. Bequeathed from father to son, this intangible cultural asset could help a family maintain elite status for decades or even centuries.

The sociologist Pierre Bourdieu sees competence in high culture as a form of "capital" that allows elite families to reproduce their privileged social status in the subsequent generation.[30] Traditionally sociologists have seen social status mostly in economic terms, emphasizing the inheritance of wealth as the mechanism perpetuating social class. Bourdieu amended this view by stressing how immaterial assets such as good taste and familiarity with high culture also tend to run in elite families, helping them preserve their privileged status. Such was the case in Song dynasty China. Cultured fathers taught their sons the abstruse details of tea connoisseurship as a way of passing down social prestige to the next generation. The usefulness of tea in maintaining literati identity helps account for their enthusiasm for this pursuit.

When literati embraced the way of tea, they endowed it with their own sensibilities, not only writing in minute detail but even enthusing about their subject in rhapsodic terms. As a result of their interests and priorities, tea culture began to diverge considerably from its early expressions in the Buddhist temples of the south. Literati also elevated its cultural standing. Su Shi and other major cultural figures saw tea drinking as a rarified pleasure worthy of the educated gentleman's full attention. Whereas the vulgar parvenu sought out gaudy and expensive indulgences, only a man of refinement could fully appreciate the simple elegance of tea.[31]

Ouyang Xiu analyzed the psychology of tea drinking in detail, demonstrating the maturity of literati connoisseurship.[32] He realized that appreciating tea consists of several aspects, as this experience affects the drinker in a number of different ways. The feelings evoked by tea constitute sentiments (*qing*), a term often contrasted with rationality or social constraints. This emotive quality makes tea drinking an extremely intimate, personal, and highly subjective experience. In particular, drinking tea evokes feelings of pleasure. However, this sort of pleasure differs from lowly hedonic gratifications such as eating or sex. Due to the web of cultured associations that enveloped tea culture, appreciating this beverage allowed the drinker to transcend base physical sensations and experience a highly refined sense of pleasure worthy of the polished aesthete.

As literati embraced a cultivated style of tea drinking, they began to deploy it in ways calculated to make their lives more elegant.[33] By doing so, they integrated tea into a much larger and more ambitious cultural

Figure 4.3. Ouyang Xiu

project. During the Song, incisive gentlemen realized that virtually every aspect of life could be aesthetically perfected, thus turning the human being into a living work of art. The Renaissance began when Italian humanists grasped a similar revelation.[34]

> The individual became a more and more carefully considered and significant cultural construct, in many ways a work of art, painted socially in a series of complex negotiations that turned around consensus realities and the various groups with which the individual lived and interacted. The key here is "negotiations," for in negotiations that people wittingly or unwittingly carried out with the groups that surrounded them in society, self-fashioning became a more nuanced and complex ongoing *social process*.

As in Europe, the insight that a person could become akin to an artwork had an incalculable impact on Chinese culture. Integrating tea into high culture gave literati a heightened awareness of human potential.

As gentlemen honed each aspect of tea culture, they did not limit their attentions to mechanical brewing and drinking techniques. Talented drinkers also raised the general tone of tea drinking by associating it closely with other refined pursuits such as art, music, and literature.[35] As a result, tea connoisseurship entered the pantheon of standard polite accomplishments expected of the gentleman. By the Song, a reputation for elegance required mastery of "go (*weiqi*), zither, calligraphy, painting, *shi* and *qu* poetry, and tea."[36] Literati often mixed these pursuits together, drinking tea while listening to music and appreciating paintings. Sometimes a group of educated friends would compose poetry over their teacups. Or perhaps a few cultured friends would sip tea while playing go.

Calligraphy provides an example of how literati integrated tea with other prestigious cultural pursuits. Because so many poets described tea in their works, and calligraphers often wrote out these verses in artistic script, tea emerged as a popular theme in calligraphy. Some of the greatest masterpieces of calligraphy from the Tang and Song dynasty mention tea. A letter written by Su Shi to a friend, suggesting they drink tea together, presents a particularly fine specimen of this practice.[37] Currently housed in the National Palace Museum in Beijing, Su's beautiful handwriting led subsequent generations to deem this casual note an artistic treasure.

But the impact of tea on literati culture did not stop here. Virtually every pursuit valued by educated gentlemen became associated with tea in one way or another. To take just one example, antique collecting became extremely popular during the Song, and poetry often links antiques with tea.[38] Whereas many connoisseurs declared a natural setting ideal for tea drinking, some literati preferred to enjoy this drink inside while surrounded by antiques. They believed that the gently worn patina of antique furniture and old objects conjured up a soothing atmosphere of cultured beauty that intensified a drinker's subjective experience.

An exchange between two cultured Song gentlemen on the relation of tea and "ink," which refers to both calligraphy and painting, shows how intimately interlinked these two cultured practices had become.[39]

> Sima Wengong discussed tea and ink with Su Shi saying, "Tea and ink are direct opposites. Tea desires the white and ink desires the black. Tea desires the heavy and ink the light. Tea desires the new and ink the aged." Su said, "High quality tea and fine ink are both fragrant. This is their shared virtue. Steadfastness is their shared conduct. For example, the Daoist immortal is swarthy and ugly, and the Confucian gentleman is fair skinned and handsome. Though different, their virtue and conduct are the same." Sima exclaimed that this was true.

While readers today might consider their metaphor-heavy dialogue strangely oblique and affected, this style of discourse seemed perfectly reasonable to Song literati, who routinely larded their discussions with colorful poetic imagery. These two accomplished literati employed concrete tropes to bind tea together with calligraphy and painting, agreeing that tea and ink constitute a natural pair. Fusing tea with ink constituted one small part of a far larger project. Ambitious gentlemen sought to link together all literati practices into a seamless whole, thereby forming a comprehensive lifestyle dedicated to refinement and personal cultivation.

The integration of tea into refined travel further demonstrates how literati sensibilities altered tea drinking. During the Tang and Song, a cultured style of travel became popular among the educated. Men of letters often journeyed to historic ruins or scenic spots to savor the complex emotions evoked by these places. While surveying the surrounding scene, they considered it fitting to drink tea.[40] Some enthusiastic drinkers even sought out places known for growing the finest tea, making them a focus of cultured travel. Famous tea fields became almost holy sites in the eyes of connoisseurs. They journeyed great distances to these celebrated places, reasoning that drinking a particular tea in its homeland would induce particularly powerful emotional reactions in the drinker.

Most importantly, tea became a major theme in the outpouring of poetry that literati produced almost constantly. To claim membership in the social and cultural elite, a man had to be able to write acceptable poetry. However, writing a proper poem required considerable training. Not only did the aspiring poet have to have accomplished the highest reaches of literacy in written Chinese, including the numerous arcane characters encountered only in poems, but they also had to familiarize themselves with the vast canon of poems by past masters. Classical Chinese poetry constituted a self-referential system, with poets showing off their knowledge and skill by evoking subtle allusions to previous poetry in their own work. As a result, full competence in this demanding form of literature required extensive reading and memorization of the poetic canon, a time-consuming task impossible for ordinary people who had to work hard all day.

The difficulty of writing good poetry lent it immense prestige, representing far more than mere literary accomplishment. The elite made an aptitude for poetic composition the most basic threshold for entering their world. Given the immense stature of poetry, fully insinuating tea into the apex of literary culture raised the status of this drink immeasurably. Once a literatus had mastered the poetic medium, he could versify with relative ease. Almost every educated person wrote numerous poems, and a huge number have been preserved. For example, readers today can still enjoy more than forty-eight thousand surviving poems written by two thousand poets from the Tang dynasty alone.

This vast body of work includes many poems dedicated to tea, and far more that mention tea in passing.[41] Song writers continued to use tea as a stock poetic theme, and some of the greatest literary figures of that era, such as Su Shi, wrote enthusiastically and repeatedly about tea.[42] This vast body of poetry represents an exhaustive compendium of information on every aspect of tea culture. Poems record in detail the numerous varieties of tea, growing, harvesting, processing, brewing, and drinking.[43] Technical essays and books about connoisseurship often included poems on the subject, presenting tea through two different literary media within the same work. Some poets came from tea producing regions or else served in the tribute tea bureaucracy, including a few major litterateurs. Firsthand exposure to tea production informed their poems, which often serve as surprisingly reliable documents about the practical side of the tea industry.

Changes in the style and content of Chinese literature facilitated the effervescence of tea poetry. Prior to the Tang, many poems took a pessimistic tone, often focusing on topics such as death. But over time, poetry had become increasingly life affirming, and poets often focused on pleasurable topics. This fundamental shift in literary sentiments paved the way for the popularity of tea poetry.[44]

Poetry about physical objects also came into vogue prior to the Tang. Even before tea emerged as a common theme, poets had already become accustomed to using physical objects to represent important feelings and ideas about the nature of existence. They utilized an object as a foil, onto which they would project subjective human feelings and concerns.[45] Before the Tang, poets had already applied this technique to plants, landscape features, animals, and even bronze vessels. Poets wrote about apparently trivial things such as trees and insects, not to provide objective descriptions but to project their own feelings upon them.[46] This fascination with physical objects facilitated the integration of tea as a major theme in mainstream poetic conventions. It also encouraged poets to think of tea in more profound terms, using the objects associated with tea drinking, and the act itself, as a vehicle for expressing their own reflections. Even descriptions of the fire and water essential to making tea could convey the innermost thoughts and feelings of the poet. The psychological depth of tea poetry enriched connoisseurship immeasurably.

In addition to mainstream poetry, writers put tea to more specialized uses as well. For example, poets who grew up in tea regions used it to express nostalgia for their hometown. To them, the scenery of tea fields and the bustle of harvesting and processing recalled their childhood.[47] Also, as gentlemen often exchanged tea as gifts, it became customary to append a poem to commemorate this present and make it more personal.[48] Connoisseurs often wrote eulogies in praise of tea to express their appreciation during a drinking session. Composing hortatory poetry ornamented the experience of drinking tea by integrating it with a cultured literary exercise. The emergence of varied types of tea poetry marks the ultimate fruition of literati tea connoisseurship, which developed far beyond mere technical mastery to merge seamlessly with art and literature.

NOTES

1. Wang He, "Tang Song gu yi chashu gouchen," *Nongye kaogu* 2 (1998): 263–68.

2. Liu Wenzhi, "'Shuipin' bianzheng," *Guji zhengli yanjiu xuekan* 6 (1995): 35–37.

3. Fang Yanshou, "Fujian zui zao de tuobenshu—Cai Xiang de 'Cha lu,'" *Yanhuang zongheng* 6 (2007): 51.

4. Liao Jianzhi, *Mingdai cha wenhua yishu* (Taipei: Xiuwei, 2007), 249–81 describes twenty-six Ming dynasty books about tea.

5. Zhao Ji, *Daguan chalun*, in *Zhongguo gudai chaye quanshu,* ed. Ruan Haogeng et al. (Hangzhou: Zhejiang sheying, 1999), 89.

6. Li Bincheng, "Tangren yu cha," *Nongye kaogu* 2 (1995): 27.

7. Zhao, *Daguan chalun,* 90.

8. Zhao, *Daguan chalun*, 93; Cai Xiang, *Chalu*, in *Zhongguo gudai chaye quanshu*, 65.

9. Ouyang Xiu, *Ouyang Xiu quanji* (Beijing: Zhonghua, 2001), vol. 1, ch. 7, p. 114.

10. By the Ming dynasty, the tea hut had been standardized. For a detailed description of the ideal tea hut see Liao, *Mingdai cha wenhua yishu*, 179.

11. Zhang Youxin, *Jiancha shuiji*, in *Zhongguo gudai chaye quanshu*, 28–30.

12. Wen Tingyun, *Caicha lu*, in *Zhongguo gudai chaye quanshu*, 37.

13. Tong Qiqing, "Tang Song shiqi Zhejiang cha wenhua de fazhan," *Nongye kaogu* 4 (1997): 28 discusses how the Zhejiang tea industry stimulated the development of local tea wares.

14. Zhao Hengfu, "Tang Song chazhan yu yincha yishu," *Wenwu shijie* 6 (2001): 49–51.

15. Li Qian, "Mantan Song cha de se xiang wei ji qi shenmei fengshang de bianhua," *Nongye kaogu* 4 (2011): 79–83.

16. Cai, *Chalu*, 65.

17. Jin Wenkai, "Songdai pincha yishu de shenmei yinsu—cong Su Dongpo de yongcha shi tanqi," *Suihua Xueyuan xuebao* 5 (2006): 62–66.

18. Zhao, *Daguan chalun*, 93.

19. Fu Lingling, "Lu You chashi yanjiu" (master's thesis, Department of Chinese, Qufu Normal University, 2006), 4–5.

20. Song Zian, *Dongxi shi chalu*, in *Zhongguo gudai chayequanshu*, 71–76.

21. Shi Shaohua, *Songdai yong chashi yanjiu* (Taipei: Wenjin, 1996), 176.

22. Zhou Feng, *Bu cha jing*, in *Zhongguo gudai chaye quanshu*, 57–58.

23. Cai, *Chalu*, 65.

24. Liao, *Mingdai cha wenhua yishu*, 239.

25. Zhao Ruicai and Zhang Zhonggang, "Zhong wan Tang cha, shi guanxi fawei," *Wenshizhe* 4 (2003): 140.

26. Huang Ru, *Pincha yaolu*, in *Zhongguo gudai chaye quanshu*, 77.

27. "Jinshi lu houxu," in Li Qingzhao, *Li Qingzhao ji jianzhu*, annot. Xu Peijun (Shanghai Shanghai guji, 2002), 310.

28. Huo Ran, *Songdai meixue sichao* (Changchun: Changchun chubanshe, 1997), 105.

29. Yu Yue and Chen Lingling, "Tang Song chashi zheli zhuiqiu zonglun," *Nongye kaogu* 5 (2010): 168; Shi, *Songdai yong chashi yanjiu*, 130.

30. Pierre Bourdieu, *Distinction: A Social Critique of the Judgement of Taste*, trans. Richard Nice (London: Routledge, 1986), 11–23.

31. Chen Yu and Du Xiaoqin, "Songdai wenren cha de rensheng zhi le," *Wenshi zhishi* 12 (2007): 93–94.

32. Yu Yue, *Chalu licheng: Zhongguo cha wenhua liubian jianshi* (Beijing: Guangming ribao, 1999), 83.

33. Fu, "Lu You chashi yanjiu," 10.

34. Guido Ruggiero, *The Renaissance in Italy: A Social and Cultural History of the Rinascimento* (Cambridge: Cambridge University Press, 2014), 326.

35. Wen Ye, "Tang Song wenyuan yu chadao wenhua," *Nongye kaogu* 2 (1995): 104–5 cites many examples from poetry.

36. Yu Wenxia, "Cong 'Daguan chalun' kan Song Huizong de cha wenhua qingjie ji Songren chadao," *Nongye kaogu* 2 (2005): 60.

37. Hu Dan, *Chayi fengqing: Zhongguo cha yu shuhua zhuanke yishu de qihe* (Beijing: Guangming ribao, 1999), 60. On pp. 54–62 Hu discusses many other famous works of calligraphy written about various aspects of tea.

38. Yu, *Chalu licheng*, 85.

39. Anonymous, *Boxue huishu*, in *Qinding siku quanshu cunmu congshu* (Taipei: Taiwan shangwu yinshuguan, 1995), vol. 3:147, p. 360 (12:74a).

40. Li, "Tangren yu cha," 23.

41. Li, "Tangren yu cha," 15 has a chart of Tang imperial reigns recording the number of poets who wrote about tea and the number of tea poems from each era. Shu Yujie, *Zhongguo cha wenhua jingo daguan* (Beijing: Dianzi gongye, 1999), 486–540 reproduces some of the most important Tang and Song poems about tea.

42. Wu Siqiang, "Su Dongpo de zhucha jing," *Cha bolan* 11 (2010): 60–61.

43. Wu Shuijin and Chen Weiming, "Song shi yu cha wenhua," *Nongye kaogu* 4 (2001): 173–75.

44. Chen and Du, "Songdai wenren cha de rensheng zhi le," 91.

45. Zhao Hongju, "Luelun Wei Jin yongwu shi de guoduxing yiyi," *Nei Menggu Daxue xuebao*, 45, no. 1 (2013): 98–101.

46. Yang Quhui, "Xikunti de xingcheng ji qi dui Songdai shifeng de kaichuang yiyi," *Changshou gaozhuan xuebao* 1 (1995): 27–30, 85.

47. Shi, *Songdai yong chashi yanjiu*, 155–58.

48. Liao, *Mingdai cha wenhua yishu*, 212–24 gives several examples.

5

MORALITY

When the monk Jiaoran started talking about the "way of tea," his choice of words imbued a formerly humble beverage with an air of profundity, encouraging people to approach tea drinking as a potentially meaningful experience. Calling tea a "way" (*dao*) implied many things. On a mundane level, the way of tea referred to a standardized set of rules for brewing and drinking. But because Daoism, Confucianism, and Buddhism all employ *dao* as a key technical term, declaring tea to be a "way" also implied that it possesses rich moral and spiritual content. While connoisseurship initially focused on technical issues such as the best types of water and the method for toasting a tea disk to perfection, literati also began to explore the moral dimension of tea drinking. In doing so, they elevated tea far beyond pleasure or aesthetics, using it as an ethical tool that could turn the drinker into a better person.

Ideas about tea can only be fully appreciated by relating them to the original intellectual context. Chinese thought took a unique direction at a very early date, so many basic ideas and assumptions differed substantially from those in other parts of the globe. The philosopher Karl Jaspers addressed the question of why the intellectual development of each of the world's major civilizations has differed so much. He noted that each culture passed through an "axial age" early in its history, a time when its essential characteristics emerged. During this sensitive era, a handful of influential figures posed key questions that thinkers of subsequent generations felt compelled to address.[1] These primal questions had an immense impact on the subsequent evolution of intellectual endeavor, as they set the boundaries of intellectual discourse. As these questions differed so much in each place, each civilization embarked down different paths of inquiry. So while thinkers in ancient India focused on religious questions and the Greeks explored logic, epistemology, and ontology, Chinese turned to pragmatic social issues. Most importantly, Chinese wondered how someone can live a good life within the context of society. Ethics thus emerged as a key concern early in Chinese intellectual history, as it regulates the individual's dealings with others. Intensive discussions of moral questions persisted over subsequent generations.

To be considered a significant intellectual topos, the way of tea had to be integrated into the matrix of moral discourse at the core of Chinese thought. Deep-thinking enthusiasts conceptualized tea in many different ways, but regardless of their mode of understanding or school of thought, they eventually linked tea with morality. Elevating this beverage into a subject of moral concern infused it with a sense of weighty importance. Connoisseurs realized that in addition to providing a subtle sensory experience and a focus of aesthetic refinement, far more consequentially tea could elicit moral introspection and improvement.

When frustrated literati turned to tea for consolation, they started to see it as a liquid imbued with moral consequence. Confucianism provided standard ideas about how the gentleman ought to seek solace. Due to the numerous setbacks that Confucius experienced in his own life, he addressed his teachings not just to the successful, but also toward those who had failed to realize their dreams despite possessing sufficient talent and rectitude. He lauded the man who cultivates himself to such a degree that he can endure poverty and other setbacks with poise and equanimity. This acquiescent worldview eventually came to be known as "content with poverty and delighting in the way" (*anpin ledao*).[2] Confucius believed that this wise attitude not only represents useful forbearance but also offers a deep insight into life's priorities. Although we usually pay attention to money and success, morality ought to be our true goal. The applicability of these insights to frustrated literati, who often struggled to maintain their integrity within a system that rewarded moral compromises, helps explain the perennial appeal of Confucianism to China's literati.

When gentlemen turned to tea for consolation, they brought it into the Confucian moral framework. This imperfect world can be an inhospitable place for people who hold themselves to the highest ethical standards. Unable to thrive in a society dominated by the unscrupulous, yet unwilling to betray their principles, they could nevertheless take solace in an awareness of their own goodness. Immersion in tea culture provided a suitable outlet for the frustrated. Both contemplative and aesthetic, the way of tea provided an appropriate escape for those seeking to preserve a commitment to the good. The unsuccessful literatus who immersed himself in this quiet pleasure could perhaps more readily accept his circumstances, however humble, thus encouraging him to remain committed to integrity.[3]

The evolution of tea drinking during Tang to Song affected its orientation within the realm of ethics.[4] Tea initially had close links to Buddhism. Monks saw it as a potential tool for self-refinement, but of course their primary objectives remained religious rather than Confucian. Beginning in the mid-Tang, secular drinking customs shifted away from mind-numbing luxury toward a more introspective style of appreciation. Literati realized that this simplified way of tea, sitting quietly and seeking self-understanding, might awaken a heightened sensitivity to virtue. As tea led the drinker toward authenticity, he might discover the innermost core of innate goodness that Mencius believed resides within each of us.

Lu Yu recognized the association between tea and virtue and made it a foundational principle of the way of tea. As tea culture developed, this moral dimension came increasingly to the forefront. For example, Emperor Song Huizong specifically linked tea with virtue, considering morality one of the beverage's major qualities. In a culture that often correlated beauty with virtue, Huizong saw the aesthetic refinement of tea as a sign of implicit ethical qualities. "Gentlemen dressed in red and commoners in course garb are blessed and moved toward virtue, as all employ elegance in undertaking tea drinking."[5] By identifying the good with the beautiful, technical connoisseurship became the starting point for a much larger project—the elevation of tea into the realm of moral philosophy.

As intellectual currents shifted, new openings emerged for assimilating tea into ethical frameworks. In particular, the rise of Neo-Confucianism, which occurred just as Song tea culture was reaching a peak of

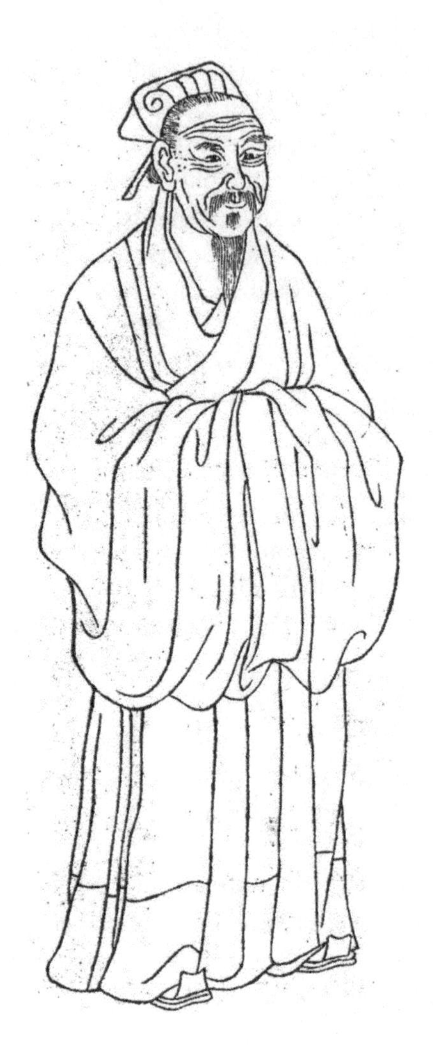

Figure 5.1. Zhu Xi

refinement, allowed drinkers to employ the way of tea as a morally uplifting enterprise.[6] Zhu Xi (1130–1200) and some other influential Neo-Confucian thinkers advocated a technique called "investigation of things" (*gewu*), which they considered a primary source of moral insight. At this time, some thinkers believed that the core principles of Confucian ethics are not the arbitrary inventions of human beings, but imitated the fundamental order constituting the natural world. Neo-Confucians believed that the regularities we see in the physical matter of the universe function in parallel with the moral principles of social order. They claimed that ancient sages had recognized these patterns by observing nature, and then enshrined these insights in the classics and Confucian canon. Because the same natural patterns still surround us, visible to anyone who cares to look for them, we can directly experience the same fundamental moral insights by "investigating things" on our own. By observing and contemplating the order implicit in the natural world, we can appreciate the objective foundation of Confucian ethics.

So how does one "investigate things"? This methodological problem became a subject of intense debate, and opinions varied considerably. Generally speaking, Song Neo-Confucians believed that an observer investigates things by examining nature and physical reality with the proper mindset. They believed that anyone who looks closely enough at his surroundings can detect the fundamental patterns that lend the material world both physical and moral order. Some patterns involve regular natural occurrences, such as the sun's unfailing appearance in the east every morning. But unlike scientific empiricism, the Neo-Confucian investigation of things did not seek to reduce the cosmos to mechanistic natural laws. They conceptualized the universe in organismic terms, believing it to consist of intertwined moral and material patterns. Because social order imitates nature, we do not have to study old books in order to understand moral principles. By looking closely at seemingly trivial details in the physical world, we can discern the grand moral patterns described by the ancient sages, as they encircle us in every direction.

Because the investigation of things demands sustained reflection, tea can aid this process. Drinking tea affects the mood, inspiring drinkers to slow down and forget daily annoyances and worries. By clearing the mind, tea also provides an ideal entrée to quiet reflection. After mentally decelerating, the philosophically minded tea man can then observe his surroundings with fresh sensitivity and begin to detect the fundamental patterns underlying physical reality. This introspective attitude can also lead the drinker to contemplate life's deeper issues, including moral problems. So tea drinking provides an effective tool for investigating things to understand the nature of reality, making it a starting point for moral cultivation. In light of the "investigation of things" method, some literati believed that consuming tea with the proper mindset can make us better people.

Zhu Xi, the greatest advocate of investigating things, used tea to demonstrate how a close examination of our surroundings can yield insights into the deeper structure of reality. Zhu noted that on a material level, natural patterns account for the flavor of tea and our basic reaction to it. The pleasure and relaxation evoked by tea drinking cannot be explained away as random reactions, as everyone has a similar experience. Zhu Xi referred to this process as a type of "way" *(dao)*.[7] He maintained that the physical qualities constituting tea's flavor do not arise haphazardly, but reflect the interaction of general regularities on our sense of taste. Even the drinker's psychological reactions to tea follow general principles. For example, the sense of calmness we feel while drinking tea cannot be dismissed as an accident. Because other people tend to have the same reaction to tea, the sense of relaxation it elicits stands as a general principle.

Having used his theories to explain the physiology and psychology of tea drinking, Zhu Xi took the matter even further by contending that we can use tea as a tool to investigate things. Zhu Xi believed that the contemplative atmosphere of tea drinking allows the observant drinker to descry the fundamental patterns shaping our world and to differentiate these fixed patterns from individual subjective feelings. "Natural patterns and human desires need to be distinguished. When we drink a bowl of tea, we can know what is natural pattern and what is human desire."[8]

Tea drinking fit perfectly into the Neo-Confucian training pioneered by Zhu Xi and his circle. To investigate things, a person has to slow down, cultivate a reflective mindset, and sit for a long time in a natural setting. Drinking tea provides all of the conditions necessary for properly investigating things. Ever since the Tang dynasty, many drinkers had sought our quiet natural spots as most conducive to appreciating tea. And because it takes time to prepare and drink, especially when made according to the complicated method favored by literati, the drinker inevitably relaxes, moves more slowly, and takes in his surroundings with heightened acuity. In this way, tea evokes a contemplative atmosphere conducive to philosophical insight.

Aside from Neo-Confucian ethics, the ritualistic aspect of tea drinking offered connoisseurs another way to link tea with morality. The

Figure 5.2. An ideal place to drink tea and investigate things

concept of ritual (*li*) covered a wide range of prescribed behavior, from formal ceremonies to everyday manners and even general deportment. Since antiquity, Confucius and other great thinkers had praised these standardized modes of behavior as vehicles for conveying and instilling goodness. They identified several uses for ritual. Because they believed that the ancients had designed the rites to express central virtues, performing a ritual actualizes this goodness in the individual. In addition to the externals of good conduct, Confucius also emphasized the psychological dimensions of ritual. If one performs a rite repeatedly, the moral values it embodies become second nature, whether or not one fully understands them. Because of the effect that ritual has upon us, it can serve as a powerful tool for personal transformation, making someone better by turning abstract virtues into automatic habits.

Many experts have remarked on the ceremonial quality of the way of tea. Although the ritual canon obviously did not include tea drinking, as it had been redacted long before tea entered China's heartland, the complicated procedures necessary for proper brewing and drinking nevertheless constituted a de facto rite. In addition, some drinkers formalized tea culture even more. As they drank, behaved, and talked with measured politesse, the tea parties of serious gentlemen could end up resembling a ceremony. Tang and Song drinkers noted the resemblance of tea drinking to the rites and began to regard it as an orthodox expression of ritual propriety.[9]

Tea's usurpation of wine's traditional ceremonial functions imbued it with even more ritualistic authority. In antiquity, fermented beverages had an intimate connection with the rites, as many ceremonies used wine as a prop. When tea replaced wine in many observances, it also took over some of the ritual and moral prestige enjoyed by that rival beverage. For example, people began using tea in ancestral sacrifices in lieu of wine, or together with it, insinuating tea into a supremely important rite.[10] Furthermore, using tea to venerate the ancestors led drinkers to associate it with filial piety, and poets even began to claim that drinking tea evoked filial sentiments.[11] Tea also became a standard component in feasts held at the Tang court in tandem with the Qingming ancestral sacrifices. During these observances, emperors and courtiers probably used the lavish tea ware unearthed at the Famen Temple, consuming this drink in a highly ritualistic manner appropriate to this solemn occasion.[12]

Tea also became a standard accouterment in other religious ceremonies and ritual occasions. For example, tea featured in the rites seeking protection from the gods and ancestors, and the emperor held a tea feast after an important religious sacrifice in the year 798.[13] When envoys visited distant lands, ritualistic niceties included gifts of tea to foreign princes. During a wedding ceremony, the bride's dowry often included tea. Tea featured in daily social rituals such as greetings, farewells, visits, and exchanges of good wishes. So as tea acquired myriad ritualistic uses, from profound religious ritual to everyday good manners, this drink became a standard feature in the major and minor ceremonies holding a civilized society together.

Ritual held a central place in Chinese views of the human being and society. The philosopher Herbert Fingarette explored the surprising implications of Chinese ideas of ritual, which he considers central to the Confucian project. While outside observers might dismiss traditional Chinese ritual as empty show, Fingarette sees it as "an emphatic, intensified and sharply elaborated extension of everyday *civilized* intercourse."[14] He argues that the rites can seem almost akin to magic, in that we can use them to accomplish important and useful things without coercion. Simply by conducting a ritual, civilized order appears. Moreover, enacting these standardized behaviors instills life with dignity and harmony. Through ritual, people realize their own humanity. In consequence, integrating tea into such an important aspect of Chinese values imbued it with moral significance.

Beyond the obvious ties between formal tea drinking and ritual propriety, some enthusiasts linked tea with other types of virtue as well. Although people today might view claims of tea's morality with skepticism, according to ideas prevalent in Chinese literati culture this association seemed perfectly reasonable. Ouyang Xiu's poetry describes the morally cultivated Confucian gentleman or "superior man" (*junzi*) as a habitual tea drinker, taking tea to symbolize the successful achievement of virtue.[15]

Beyond ritual, tea evoked other moral resonances as well. A poem about ideal family values by the cultural polymath Huang Tingjian (1045–1105), famed for both his outstanding poetry and calligraphy, links tea with family values. Mentioning the fame of Confucius and Mencius, he pays tribute to the virtues that maintain family harmony. Then he evokes the properly ordered family by describing each member carrying out their proper role, culminating with an image of the studious gentleman brewing tea to drink while he reads.[16] Through the imagery in this poem, Huang takes tea drinking to symbolize moral respectability.

More subtle ethical correspondences grew out of the Confucian tendency to find moral significance in aesthetic distinctions. Gentlemen often judged taste and behavior as either elegant (*ya*) or vulgar (*su*). At first glance, these terms seem purely aesthetic. However, literati believed that goodness usually seems beautiful while evil appears ugly and vulgar in comparison. According to these assumptions, because the literati way of tea unquestionably expresses elegance, it constitutes a method for refining the self and therefore embodies virtue.[17]

The line between elegance and vulgarity is not always clear-cut. Su Shi and Huang Tingjian carried aesthetics to a new level of sophistication by declaring that sometimes we should "take the vulgar as elegant" (*yi su wei ya*).[18] This revisionist assessment of beauty called for a radical reexamination of aesthetic values. These cultured gentlemen realized that common or trivial items could become elegant if used correctly. Their reassessment of aesthetics justified taking tea, an everyday beverage, and making it an orthodox subject for poetry, painting, calligraphy, and other cultured pursuits.

As tea increasingly replaced wine in social contexts, people often contrasted the two drinks with each other. And whenever they put the two side by side, tea appeared far more virtuous in comparison. Unlike alcohol, tea drinking exemplifies quiet moderation and harmony.[19] Nor did connoisseurs consider temperate tea drinking simply relaxing. Since antiquity, ethical discourse had extolled social and mental balance as virtuous in itself. Confucian thinkers accordingly put forward moderation (*zhongyong*) as a lofty ideal. They held that extreme emotions and behavior tend to block the seamless integration of the individual with society, hindering the ultimate goal of the Confucian project. Anything that extinguishes these antisocial extremes can aid moral cultivation.

It so happens that tea performs just this sort of function. To prepare tea, we must patiently wait for water to boil and leaves to steep. The drinker must patiently carry out set procedures in a fixed order, making tea akin to a ritual even when consumed informally among good friends. This measured process inevitably induces a sense of inner calm, presenting the gentlemen with a valuable method for nurturing the Confucian virtue of measured moderation.

The culture that grew up around wine lauded passion and strong feelings, making the quiet reflectiveness elicited by tea seem calm and restrained in comparison. Yet in spite of the opposite psychological tones enveloping wine and tea culture, both could awaken a feeling of melancholy, literally a "bitter heart" (*kuxin*).[20] Although this state of mind sounds unpleasant, Chinese men of letters prized it. A sense of melancholy forces us to look beyond our daily routine and gaze more deeply into the disturbing abyss of human experience. As a result, melancholic introspection can elicit ethical insights, thereby intensifying individual moral cultivation.

Another moral quality involves the "frugal simplicity" (*jianpu*) that Lu Yu considered essential to the way of tea. Although outwardly similar to the spirit of calm essential for embracing the Confucian doctrine of the mean, Lu's frugal simplicity owes more to Zen values.[21] This humble ideal helps explain why Lu Yu wanted to turn tea culture away from ostentatious luxury. This key shift in tea culture involved far more than just asserting a new aesthetic or taste. In rejecting extravagance, Lu cast off the shallow pursuit of social status and instead used tea to pursue deep moral and transcendental goals. While his initial inspiration for this view may have been Buddhist, this new philosophical direction made tea amenable to the cultivation of Confucian ethics as well.

When reduced to the absolute basics, tea consists of nothing more than the dried leaves of a bitter herb steeped in hot water. Something this simple can easily arouse a sense of frugality in the drinker. And ever since antiquity, thinkers of various schools of thought had lauded frugality as a virtue. Historians even pointed to wastefulness and drunkenness as a major cause for the catastrophic collapse of ancient dynasties. So to thinkers immersed in Confucianism, obsession with luxury implies more than just superficiality. Such a shallow state of mind can also make people cruel and wicked. To avoid this fate, we can drink tea in a deliberately simple manner that induces quiet reflection. In this way, frugal tea drinking can become a platform for profound moral cultivation.

After simplicity became the standard mode for literati tea drinking, many connoisseurs began to laud tea for its purity (*qing*). Although ancient thinkers often associated purity with Daoism, Confucianism inspired tea men to value this quality as well. After Lu Yu reformed tea culture, drinking sessions became increasingly quiet, simple, and natural. Literati interpreted this atmosphere as embodying purity. Tang dynasty poets often mention purity (*qing*) in relation to tea. And connoisseurs saw natural places, notable for their purity, as suitable for producing and drinking fine tea.[22] Confucians had long emphasized the link between humanity and nature, which is embodied by heaven.[23] So seeking out natural venues to drink tea brings us closer to heaven itself.

Tea experts extended this line of thought to encompass a metaphorical purity as well. To connoisseurs, purity represented a high aesthetic ideal.[24] For example, *An Account of Tea* (*Cha shu*), an early book on the subject by Pei Wen, a friend of Lu Yu, describes this drink as pure, clean, and harmonious, concluding that we should consider tea uniquely elevated due to these virtuous characteristics.[25] Song dynasty works continued to promote this viewpoint, often mentioning purity as a prime quality of tea. Sometimes purity constituted a literal physical quality that makes tea taste and smell good. However, purity could also imply higher ideals as well. Beyond simple aesthetics, purity could be extended to encompass a heightened moral state. To connoisseurs, the purity of tea seemed akin to Confucianism's unblemished integrity. In this way they furnished a physical and aesthetic ideal with a moral dimension.[26]

A painting by Qian Xuan (1235–1305) called "Lu Tong Brewing Tea" visualizes the ideal of purity in tea.[27] The artist's frustrating personal experiences informed his painting. Although Qian trained to serve as an official under the Southern Song, after the Mongols conquered China he refused public service out of loyalty to the previous dynasty. During his forced retirement he devoted himself to painting. In this work, Qian depicts the famous Tang dynasty hermit Lu Tong (790–835), another talented gentleman who suffered the same misfortune of living through a chaotic era. By painting this historic recluse, the artist alludes to the difficulties and frustrations that marked his own life.

Despite his erudition and connections, Lu Tong had also refused to serve in government. Instead he retired to a mountainous region and devoted himself to tea and poetry. Qian seems to have been inspired by one of Lu's poems, which includes the line "the fifth bowl [of tea] purifies my flesh and bones," which associates tea drinking with a pursuit of personal purity in spite of the misfortune of living during a

Figure 5.3. "Lu Tong Brewing Tea" by Qian Xuan (Courtesy of National Palace Museum, Taipei)

decadent age. Lu Tong's travails, and the transcendental quest it inspired, clearly resonated with the artist. As this painting reveals, Qian felt enormous admiration for an exceptional gentleman who turned to tea as a refuge from the corruptions of power.

This painting of an idealistic hermit ties tea drinking with the long and respected tradition of eremitism. By linking tea to this moralistic movement, Qian fostered yet another ethical element in the increasingly reflective culture surrounding this beverage. Qian's association of principled reclusion with tea appears far from anomalous, and in fact conforms to the general spirit of his age. During the Song, it became common for literati and even officials to affect the same sort of taste as recluses, and this style of aesthetics gained considerable prestige. To them, drinking tea in a way that consciously evoked eremitism made this pursuit seem more beautiful, refined, profound, and even virtuous.[28] In many ways, tea had become a powerful tool for pursuing moral improvement.

NOTES

1. Karl Jaspers, *The Origin and Goal of History*, trans. Michael Bullock (London: Routledge, 1953), 1–21.
2. Fan Ye, *Hou Hanshu*, annot. Liu Zhao and Li Xian et al. (Beijing: Zhonghua shuju, 1965), 26:917.
3. Chen Yu and Du Xiaoqin, "Tang Song wenren cha de wenhua yiwen ji qi xingcheng guocheng," *Qinghua Daxue xuebao* 6 (2007): 39–40.
4. Yu Yue and Chen Lingling, "Tang Song chashi zheli zhuiqiu zonglun," *Nongye kaogu* 5 (2010): 166.
5. Zhao Ji, *Daguan chalun*, in *Zhongguo gudai chaye quanshu,* ed. Ruan Haogeng et al. (Hangzhou: Zhejiang sheying, 1999), 89.
6. Yu and Chen, "Tang Song chashi zheli zhuiqiu zonglun," 167.
7. Li Jingde (ed.). *Zhuzi yulei*, annot. Wang Xingxian (Beijing: Zhonghua shuju, 1986), 138:3294.
8. Li, *Zhuzi yulei*, 36:963.
9. Huang Chang, *Yinshan ji*, in *Qinding Siku quanshu* (Taipei: Taiwan shangwu, n.d.), vol. 1.1283, 4:3a–4a; Li Fei, "Tang Song chadao daxing zhi yuanyin fenxi," *Sichuan Ligong Xueyuan xuebao* 25, no. 3 (2010): 64.
10. Li, *Zhuzi yulei*, 90:2314, 107:2674.
11. Shi Shaohua, *Songdai yong chashi yanjiu* (Taipei: Wenjin, 1996), 150–53.
12. Gong Zhi, *Zhongguo gongcha* (Hangzhou: Zhejiang sheying), 33.
13. Zhu Nailiang, "Tangdai cha wenhua yu Lu Yu 'Chajing,'" *Nongye kaogu* 2 (1995): 59; Li Bincheng, "Tangren yu cha," *Nongye kaogu* 2 (1995): 22–23; Fang Jian, "Tang Song chali chasu shulue," *Minsu yanjiu* 4 (1998): 74–75;

Guan Jianping, *Cha yu Zhongguo wenhua* (Beijing: Renmin, 2001), 217–20; Zhou Hui, "Chali xingcheng yuanyin shulun," *Shenyang Hangkong Gongye Xueyuan xuebao* 23, no. 6 (2006): 88–90; Wang Guoan and Yao Ying, *Cha yu Zhongguo wenhua* (Shanghai: Hanyu dacidian, 2000), 43–45; Gong, *Zhongguo gongcha*, 30.

14. Herbert Fingarette, *Confucius: The Secular as Sacred* (New York: Harper &Row, 1972), 11.

15. Lai Gongou, *Cha zhe rui zhi* (Beijing: Guangming ribao, 1999), 49–51.

16. Yu and Chen, "Tang Song chashi zheli zhuiqiu zonglun," 165.

17. Lai, *Cha zhe rui zhi,* 52–54.

18. Shi, *Songdai yong chashi yanjiu*, 77.

19. Lai, *Cha zhe rui zhi,* 60–74.

20. Xie Baocheng, "Xie 'Li Bai yu Du Fu' de 'kuxin' guyi," *Guo Moruo xuekan* 2 (2012): 60–63; Zhao Ruicai and Zhang Zhonggang, "Zhong wan Tang cha, shi guanxi fawei," *Wenshizhe* 4 (2003): 143.

21. Lu Jianwei, "Lu Yu sixiangzhong de chanxing yixiang," *Huzhou S hizhuan xuebao* 2 (1996): 54; Guan, *Cha yu Zhongguo wenhua*, 348–62.

22. Liao Jianzhi, *Mingdai cha wenhua yishu* (Taipei: Xiuwei, 2007), 210.

23. Huo Ran, *Songdai meixue sichao* (Changchun: Changchun chubanshe, 1997), 32.

24. Lai, *Cha zhe rui zhi,* 15–16; Zhao and Zhang, "Zhong wan Tang cha, shi guanxi fawei," 141–43.

25. Pei Wen, *Chashu*, in *Zhongguo gudai chaye quanshu*, 26.

26. Wang Xinxing, "Cha yu Songren shang 'qing' de meixueguan," *Jingchu Ligong Xueyuan xuebao* 25, no. 10 (2010): 46–48.

27. "Lu Tong peng cha tu." See Song Houling, "Chahua, chahua," *Gugong wenwu yuekan* 4 (1983): 104–5.

28. Chen Yu and Du Xiaoqin, "Songdai wenren cha de rensheng zhi le," *Wenshi zhishi* 12 (2007): 95; Lai, *Cha zhe rui zhi,* 32–46.

6

TRANSCENDENCE

As the culture enveloping tea evolved, steadily accruing layers of significance, enthusiasts eventually imbued their favorite drink with transcendental aspirations. The elevation of tea beyond the mundane realm began by associating it with the natural environment. Prevalent Chinese views of nature facilitated this link. Since the early medieval era, some gentlemen had claimed that even when they were preoccupied with burdensome official duties, their heart remained ensconced among mountains and forests. They saw nature not just as material reality, but also as a subjective psychological state. Inspired by Daoism, literati took this expansive view of the natural world as both refuge and model. It became common for educated men to contemplate nature, seek out beautiful natural settings, and strive to insinuate aspects of nature within themselves.[1] According to this way of thinking, when we consider something truly profound we ought to relate it to the natural world and then integrate this insight into our own mind. This subjective view of nature exerted substantial influence on Tang and Song culture, and helps explain the intimate association of tea with nature in the Chinese imagination.

From the very beginnings of tea poetry, litterateurs often conjured up scenes of natural beauty as the ideal setting for enjoying this drink. Nature appreciation became a staple theme of the genre, featuring in thousands of tea poems. For example, the poet Qian Qi describes himself sitting among bamboos, idly gazing at passing clouds, and listening to the buzz of cicadas, all while savoring the flavor of tea.[2] Lu You wrote poems that describe drinking tea in a variety of natural settings: at night surrounded by winter chrysanthemums, listening to the wind soughing through limbs of pine trees, and soothed by the babbling water of a nearby spring.[3]

Linking tea with the natural world had several inspirations. In the early years of connoisseurship, when monks first elevated tea into a cultured pursuit, many monasteries happened to occupy spots of great scenic beauty. Moreover, the Buddhist faithful traditionally sought out natural beauty as the appropriate backdrop for spiritual cultivation, exerting a profound influence on the secular elite.[4] So when insightful literati began to regard tea as a civilized activity, they often consumed it in a natural spot in imitation of Buddhist models. As the way of tea developed over the centuries, gentlemen increasingly appreciated the naturalistic side of connoisseurship and sought out beautiful environments to heighten their drinking experience. Natural beauty thus became a standard milieu for drinking sessions. Seeking out gorgeous natural settings also demonstrated a gentleman's good taste, helping to earn him a reputation as a true connoisseur.

The appropriation of traditional wine culture linked tea even more closely with nature. Poets had long depicted drunkenness positively as a way to liberate oneself from social constraints and brood about the nature of existence. As tea culture usurped wine in importance, it inherited these established conventions. Because a natural setting felt removed from humanity, it inspired a drinker to feel emancipated from burdensome social obligations and presented a perfect setting for moody introspection.[5] By appropriating these associations from the highly developed culture of alcohol, the way of tea became increasingly profound. Drinkers began to assume that tea allows us to escape troublesome responsibilities, transcend our superficial perspective on the world, and attain a heightened state of awareness.

Construction of humble teahouses in a naturalistic style became increasingly common.[6] A garden, often done up in the elegant Jiangnan fashion popular in Suzhou and other prosperous southern cities, made the ideal spot for a little tearoom. Literati envisioned themselves drinking tea while surrounded by miniature faux mountains, strange rocks, and water features. To fit in with nature, wealthy men constructed tearooms so simple that they almost seemed like the hut of an impoverished peasant. Studiously avoiding any trace of architectural ostentation enhanced the prevailing atmosphere of naturalism that literati considered ideal for tea and other cultured activities.

The convergence of nature appreciation with tea culture had a major impact on Chinese aesthetics. Tastemakers declared the natural spots associated with tea to be particularly beautiful, and literati journeyed there specifically to enjoy the view—while drinking tea, of course. Gentlemen also declared the tea tree a particularly attractive plant, and a productive agricultural landscape of hills or mountains covered with carefully tended tea hedges now counted as gorgeous scenery.[7] Mountains planted with large numbers of tea trees became revered as "tea mountains" (*chashan*) renowned for their beauty.[8] Literati began to view certain tea fields as not just beautiful but culturally and even historically significant, imbuing them with multiple layers of meaning.

Even the reputation of springs famed for good tea water became revered as important natural sites, and poets praised their beautiful natural settings.[9] It became common for literati to seek out famous springs specifically to drink tea there, considering this a refined leisure activity. In an age when travel inevitably involved hardship and discomfort, undertaking a journey just to search out good tea water demonstrated a serious commitment to connoisseurship. Remote springs also had attractive natural surroundings ideal for appreciating tea.

The high reputation of springs and mountains connected with tea inspired literati to undertake a new kind of cultured travel. Wherever a dedicated drinker went, he would bring along a full battery of tea implements and seek out gorgeous natural spots, searching far and wide for the perfect place to savor a bowl of tea. Lu Yu admits to the difficulty of traveling to remote places with an elaborate tea equipage in tow. "Further if one is trying to escape the brambles; if he is scrambling up a steep cliff; or if he is faced with pulling himself by a rope ladder up into a mountain cave to heat and grind his tea, he may pass over the roller, brush and grinder."[10] This passage hints at the travails endured by enthusiastic tea men as they clamored up steep mountain trails in search of the perfect place to brew tea.

Once tea fused with nature in the literati imagination, inspiring poetry and profound reflection, they took this transcendental viewpoint even further and began to use tea as a tool for spiritual cultivation. In the minds of many gentlemen, the atmosphere of spirituality conjured up by tea drinking remained inchoate. For example, the poetry of Lu

You often depicts tea as a way to cast off the restrictive bonds of society and experience a general sense of transcendence and higher metaphysical states.[11] Although broadly spiritual, the exact nature of this quasi-religious experience remained unelaborated. Lu may have used tea to transcend the ordinary world and enter a higher state of consciousness, but his feelings remained nebulous.

Others applied the aura of transcendentalism enveloping tea to specific problems. Given the sense of mental liberation that tea drinking could evoke, many gentlemen devoted themselves to this pursuit after they retired. They considered tea a worthy pastime for their golden years, not only due to the dignity enveloping tea culture, but also for its use as a medium for reflecting on profound matters beyond the ken of the visible world.[12] They also believed that tea allows us to temporarily escape from existential anxiety. By fostering a psychological state beyond ordinary daily cares, for a few moments the drinker can forget about the finitude of life.[13] This mental refuge provides particularly welcome consolation for the elderly, who are more likely to muse about the inevitability of death. The resulting otherworldly state of mind can even seem akin to the introspection and otherworldliness evoked by religious ritual.

The inclusion of tea in numerous ceremonies intensified the air of spirituality. As tea replaced alcohol in religious and secular rites, people increasingly assumed that it had potent supernatural powers. Even prior to the release of Lu Yu's classic text, tea already featured in sacrifices to various gods and ancestors. The appearance of tea as a standard prop in conventional religious worship imbued it with a broad sense of spiritual significance that the religious-minded gradually explored and exploited.

Daoism provided the most obvious common ground between tea and organized spirituality.[14] This way of thought glorifies the natural world, taking it as an ideal template for humans to emulate. So after tea had become intimately linked to nature in the literati imagination, it inexorably became associated with Daoist sensibilities as well. Indeed, the association of tea with Daoism dates to the beginnings of sophisticated connoisseurship when tea experts began talking about a *dao* of tea.

The writings of Lu Yu had enormous influence in this regard, as he repeatedly mentions Daoists and Daoism in *The Classic of Tea*. For example, he relates the story of a man who went into the mountains to pick tea and came upon a Daoist priest. At the cleric's suggestion, the farmer conducted a sacrifice to some wild tea trees. Afterward the trees became unusually productive and everyone in the area enjoyed their bountiful harvest.[15] This and similar tales in Lu's work, often tinged with elements of the supernatural drawn from popular supernatural literature of the time, convey his conviction that connoisseurs should appreciate and explore the Daoist side of tea.

The insightful monk Jiaoran encouraged Lu Yu's interest in Daoism. Jiaoran had clearly studied the Daoist classics, as was common among educated Tang Buddhists. He brought these ideas to bear on tea appreciation, and his tea poetry displays many Daoist motifs. For example, one poem depicts immortals who disdain fine delicacies, relying on tea for their sustenance. After consuming this magical liquid, they grow wings and ascend beyond the mundane world. Tea cures their ailments and alleviates any feelings of depression. According to this poem, tea can bring about happy longevity and even immortality.[16] In making these exaggerated claims for the benefits of tea, Jiaoran built upon common preconceptions. Tea had always enjoyed a reputation as a healthy tonic. In the hands of Daoist-inspired writers, however, this drink became far more efficacious. Not only could tea serve as a general panacea, but it also lengthened life and cleansed the mind of cares.

Later writers continued to expound on the Daoist aspects of tea. Some merely evoked general connotations by associating tea with Daoist qualities such as purity and humility. When a gentleman drank tea in a simple manner amid natural surroundings, enjoying the simple flavor and carefree atmosphere, he participated in Daoist-style aesthetics, whether consciously or not. More overt associations emerged as well. Most importantly, the humble frugality (*jian*) that Lu Yu stressed as one of tea's main merits offered a clear link with Daoism. In contrast to the sensuality inherent in alcohol or fine food, tea drinking feels innately simple. Chinese writers have praised this sort of frugality since high antiquity. The authors of the *Classic of Documents* (*Shangshu*), which includes sections dating to the eleventh century BCE, famously viewed frugality and moderation as the essential grounding for a good society, repeatedly warning that extravagance can bring down a dynasty.

In the Daoist context, frugality took on far more profound connotations. The Daoist classics, most notably the *Daodejing*, look to plain simplicity (*pu*) as a lofty ideal, a concept that had a major influence on Zen Buddhism as well. Although the pursuit of *pu* might seem unambitious, Daoists took it as an important goal of the spiritual life. They believed that casting off artificial pretenses and arbitrary social conventions allows us to realize our original self and thereby return to primal authenticity. The simple style of tea drinking, popularized by Lu Yu and carefully refined by successive generations of connoisseurs, fits perfectly with this Daoist vision of life. Drinking tea in a spirit of deliberate frugality and humility conjures up an atmosphere of unadorned simplicity that Daoists looked to as a way to transcend social conventions and seek the real self.

Daoist imagery became a staple of tea poetry. Authors who wanted to imbue a poem with meaning or beauty would often evoke immortals, longevity, distant holy mountains, and other stereotypical Daoist tropes.[17] Rather than putting hope in a heavenly afterlife, Daoists usually sought to lengthen their lifespan and purify this world into a kind of earthly paradise. To achieve these ends, Daoists searched for elixirs of longevity or even immortality, compounding exotic alchemical potions out of exotic herbs and even ingesting deadly compounds such as mercury. Because tea already had a reputation for healthy restorative powers, some poets declared it to be the long-sought Daoist panacea—a draught of immortality. In a famous poem, Li Bai extravagantly proclaims tea to be Daoist elixir, setting down a popular literary precedent that generations of epigones dutifully imitated.[18]

Tea drinking became duly integrated into Daoist spiritual practices. Although Buddhism had the closest links with tea culture, many sources also mention Daoist clerics (*daoshi*) drinking tea. Devout Daoists practiced various types of introspection and meditation as part of their religious discipline, so quietly drinking a bowl of tea helped relax them in preparation for a session of calm sitting.[19] To Daoists, tea served as a useful tool for inducing a psychological state conducive to receiving spiritual insight. Daoists considered tea so important that some even claimed that after death, when people migrated to a different realm, they continued to drink tea.[20] For how could a place possibly be paradise without tea?

Although tea became integrated into various religious rituals and practices, Buddhist monks embraced it most enthusiastically, and they had a major role in elevating tea drinking into a cultured social performance. The Tang marked the high point of Chinese Buddhism, a time when the faith reached an apex of sophistication, intellectual profundity, and influence. Buddhism had an immense impact on virtually all aspects of Tang high culture, including tea. In the early years of secular connoisseurship, when a few insightful drinkers began to grasp its potential intellectual and cultural significance, Buddhist monasteries and temples had already embraced the way of tea. Jiaoran and other poets mention "mountain monks" (*shanseng*) who not only drank and appreciated tea, but also grew, picked, and processed it.[21] For example, a monk called Chengtian lived in the mountains of Jian'an, home to the finest imperial tribute teas. There he grew a variety notable for its fine fragrance and sweetness.[22] Nor was tea production limited to a few hermit monks. Extensive fields of tea covered the mountains surrounding many famous temples, a sight so common that tea hedges assumed a religious connotation. A number of poems also describe "tea smoke" (*chayan*) created by the wood fires used to boil tea water as a common sight at mountain temples. Clouds of smoke wafting up from the temple signaled that monks inside were preparing to drink tea. Many Tang and Song monasteries even had a special teahouse (*chaliao*) or tea hall (*chatang*), attesting to the presence of tea in everyday monastic life.[23]

Early on, monks at certain mountain temples, located in areas suited for growing tea, assumed the role of tea experts. Many poems depict these pioneering connoisseurs as deeply knowledgeable about tea lore.[24] Their interest and discernment, at a time when most people still regarded tea as nothing more than vegetable soup, gave the nascent tea industry a huge boost. They raised the quality of tea and spread production over a much wider area. Wherever Buddhist monks went, they planted tea. And because monks demanded fine tea, they stimulated the development of a much better product.

The four famous mountains associated with Chinese Buddhism include Mt. Jiuhua in present-day Anhui province. Temples there played a major role in the early history of tea, as the terrain and climate happen to be perfectly suited for growing fine leaves.[25] Ever since the Tang dynasty, this mountain has yielded famous brews, including so-called furry peak (*maofeng*) tea that drinkers today still appreciate. Monks at the temples on Mt. Jiuhua earned a reputation as passionate tea men. Not only did they drink tea themselves, but they also offered it to images of the Buddha and served it to pilgrims and travelers, thereby publicizing their local product.[26] Nor were the monks of Mt. Jiuhua at all unusual in this regard. Even in the capital, Buddhist clerics took a leading role in court tea drinking, which accounts for the discovery of elaborate court tea wares at the Famen Temple.

Clerical tea drinking customs developed in parallel with practices common among laypeople. Originally monks concocted rich brews redolent with fragrant herbs, spices, and dried fruits. Then they switched to an unadulterated drink. The highly structured monastery environment supported a culture of connoisseurship. Monks accrued information about tea varieties, agriculture, processing, and drinking, and then passed it down from master to disciple alongside religious wisdom.[27] Clerics had a hand in the development and perfection of some of the most famous types of tea enjoyed during the Tang and Song. Moreover, as some monks labored in the fields themselves, they gained practical experience that gave them an unusual firsthand familiarity with production that informed their appreciation.

In addition to the tea grown at temples, monks frequently had the opportunity to taste fine teas from different places. Because Buddhist clerics had a reputation for being enthusiastic tea drinkers, it became common to offer them presents of tea.[28] Laypeople who visited temples customarily presented the residents with gifts to symbolize their piety. The emperor also routinely handed out tribute disks to major monasteries as a symbol of his personal devotion, allowing monks to enjoy some of the best tea available. Because the clerics at favored temples enjoyed a variety of fine teas, some holy places became renowned centers of tea culture. Gentlemen would visit with the express intention of enjoying good tea provided by hospitable monks. While drinking together, clerical and secular tea experts could swap opinions and information, cross-fertilizing their respective circles of connoisseurship.

During the fourth and fifth centuries, monks in southern China already drank tea regularly, making them some of the earliest tea enthusiasts.[29] Tea seems to have infiltrated the *sangha* so quickly because the monastic code prohibited alcohol to clerics and even strongly discouraged its consumption by laypeople, out of concern that drunkenness might promote immoderate behavior and the empty pursuit of carnal pleasure.[30] Even legitimate medicinal uses of alcohol gave rise to soul searching among monks.[31] Moreover, because Buddhism promotes purification of the mind and meditation, believers had to forgo any drink that clouds awareness.

Because wine had traditionally played such an important role in Chinese social interactions and religious ritual, early Buddhists found the ban on alcohol inconvenient. The importation of tea plants from distant regions of the far south provided an ideal solution to this annoying problem. Buddhists simply substituted tea for wine, using it in the same way in many contexts. A poem by Jiaoran depicts tea as a tool of spiritual life, pronouncing it far superior to the alcoholic drinks imbibed by the vulgar.[32] His startling depiction of wine as coarse and crude did not just reject the cultural status quo, but turned previous stereotypes upside down. For centuries, poets and gentlemen had lauded the consumption of alcohol as an elegant pursuit, associating it with refined activities and deep philosophical insight. Jiaoran flatly rejected the conventional assessment. In place of wine, he takes tea as the new standard of elegance and transcendence.

Tea perfectly suited the unique Buddhist lifestyle, particularly in Zen monasteries where religious practice centered on intense meditation.[33] Zen had already become an important school of Chinese Buddhism prior to the popularization of tea drinking. Because monks of that sect adopted cultured tea drinking before it became widespread among literati, they exerted considerable influence on the early genesis of the way of tea. Elite Zen monks had frequent interactions with educated laymen and members of the imperial court, making them well placed to spread their innovative views on tea.

Even so, as Buddhism discourages both attachment to worldly things and intense emotions, the passion for tea among clerics threatened to contravene their Buddhist beliefs. For monks, tea held out spiritual promise but also carried inherent dangers. If undertaken with an attitude of detachment and moderation, tea drinking could further transcendental insight, but should the love of tea become an intense desire, this craving would contravene the Buddhist spirit of detachment.

At the time, strict monastic rules forbade eating after noon. Even so, monks were still allowed to drink tea. As consuming this "drink" included sucking down the ground leaves at the bottom of the bowl, tea constituted a de facto food that could assuage hunger in the afternoon. Moreover, for clerics limited to a strict vegetarian diet, the rich tea consumed in early times, often adulterated with various additives, constituted a healthy nutritional supplement. Tea held many other attractions for Zen monks as well. It aided digestion after meals. And monks also believed that its famed medicinal qualities helped prevent sickness. Men living in such close proximity welcomed a healthy tonic that might prevent the outbreak of communicable illnesses. Importantly, some Buddhists believed that tea suppressed sexual desire. Whether or not this is actually the case, tea's early reputation as an antiaphrodisiac appealed to men sworn to celibacy.

The stimulating effects of caffeine encouraged meditation by keeping practitioners awake. Although Chinese Buddhists today rarely spend much time meditating, Zen monks of the Tang emphasized intense meditation as a central spiritual discipline. They welcomed an invigorating drink that could keep the practitioner alert and awake for periods of quiet sitting. And as temples often held meditation sessions in the afternoon and evening, tired monks welcomed a burst of caffeine. Some even saw tea alone as sufficient to sustain them during intensive meditation sessions. For example, the respected Zen master Jiangmo skipped meals and sleep entirely during long stretches of meditation, subsisting entirely on tea.[34]

Laymen associated tea drinking with Buddhist meditation, and numerous poems depict tea as a standard accouterment for the serious meditator. The saying "tea and meditation have the same flavor" (*cha chan yi wei*) sums up this association.[35] Scholars today dispute the original meaning of this terse statement. It seems to suggest that tea can transport the drinker beyond the constraints of rational thought processes to a higher state of consciousness. So like meditation, tea drinking undertaken with the proper mindset can also engender a kind of enlightenment.[36]

The idea that tea drinking can become a type of Buddhist practice lent this beverage additional appeal. The poet Bai Juyi, for example, seems to have been extremely attracted to the Buddhist style of tea. Although a layman, he nevertheless considered himself a serious Buddhist devotee. He observed certain Buddhist disciplines, practiced religious rites, and referred to himself as a "pious layman in the fragrant mountains" (*xiangshan jushi*), a designation that conveyed his devotion to Buddhism together with its intertwined tea culture.[37] Other literati also used tea as an entrée to serious Buddhist practice, or at least as a way to dabble in spirituality.

The association of tea with Buddhism presented gentlemen with yet another way to gain prestige.[38] By drinking tea amid natural surroundings with a Buddhist frame of mind, they could stake a claim to spirituality and otherworldliness without having to actually endure the strictures of monastic life. The appeal of Buddhist-affiliated tea drinking eventually extended beyond China's borders to influence Korea and Japan, stimulating the emergence of sophisticated tea cultures in countries farther east.[39] Many aspects of the famed Japanese tea ceremony originated in Buddhist tea culture imported from China.

Tea poetry frequently evokes Buddhism, the meditative Zen school in particular. Beyond describing pretty temple scenes, poets sometimes delved deeper into the topic to explore how tea can further Buddhist practice. Many poets saw Buddhist-style tea drinking as an expression of "neither immersing oneself in the world nor escaping it" (*buji buli*).[40] As a literatus drank tea, he remained part of the world. Because laypeople drank tea all the time, it could not be properly considered a religious practice ipso facto. Nevertheless, some gentlemen realized that reflective and mindful drinking can cultivate an introspective attitude, ultimately allowing someone to see the world through new eyes, thereby achieving a degree of wisdom comparable to that gained through meditation.

The air of profundity enveloping the Buddhist way of tea intrigued many literati, and they frequently sought out learned monks as partners for drinking and conversation. The friendship between Lu Yu and the "poetic monk" (*shiseng*) Jiaoran, who drank together and exchanged poems, exemplifies these interactions between elite members of the religious and secular realms. When Jiaoran coined the term "way of tea" (*chadao*), his highly suggestive choice of words evoked not just standard rules, but also moral content and even spiritual associations. Jiaoran's elevation of tea into a "way" clearly struck a chord with Lu Yu, who integrated this point of view into his own monumental work.

Many other gentlemen befriended erudite monks as well. Bai Juyi similarly enjoyed composing poetry and discussing religious matters with the cultivated monk Taoguang while they drank tea together at a scenic monastery.[41] Poets often depicted themselves drinking tea with a monk in the evening. They assumed that these sessions had special

Figure 6.1. Monk and gentleman drinking tea together

significance that went beyond the pleasures of like-minded companionship, using this setting to convey aesthetic or spiritual insights to the reader.[42] Frequent and intense interaction between literati and educated clerics fostered considerable convergence between secular and Buddhist tea culture. Some temples heartily welcomed literati, who appreciated fine tea and congenial companionship. While there, monks and laymen would enjoy civilized pleasures together. Some monasteries also had accumulated significant collections of calligraphy and painting that the monks would display to visiting gentlemen while they enjoyed tea. Monks and laymen might also spend time arranging flowers, playing go, and enjoying competitive tea games.[43]

Jiaoran famously declared that the capacity to appreciate tea singles someone out as a person worth befriending. It did not matter if the drinker was a monk or layman. Tea could bring the two realms together. Jiaoran advanced this belief in a famous poem.[44]

> At a monastery on Mt. Jiuri,
> chrysanthemums by the eastern rail are also yellow.
> So many laypeople drift around on wine.
> Who gains release and succor from the fragrance of tea?

Located in the heart of Fujian tea country, Mt. Jiuri made an ideal setting for this poem. However, describing the temple surrounded by chrysanthemums presents a somewhat unusual scene, as poets conventionally associated Buddhism with the lotus. The chrysanthemum evoked the spirit of secular recluses such as Tao Qian, and in fact Jiaoran's reference to the "eastern rail" refers specifically to one of

Tao's most famous works. So by appropriating traditional transcendental imagery and placing it in a very different context, Jiaoran draws a clear parallel between the monks in a temple surrounded by chrysanthemums and secular recluses. Even so, Jiaoran rejects Tao's drunken escapism. Instead he advocates tea as a way to untie our bonds to the world and escape the limits of arbitrary convention. By rapidly introducing a series of evocative images and references, this densely packed poem builds a bridge between tea drinking monks and like-minded literati companions. When drinking tea together, they all become akin to secular recluses. Although clerics and laymen may have different social roles, drinking tea temporarily unites them in a common quest for spiritual transcendence.

NOTES

1. Zhao Hui, *Liuchao shehui wenhua xintai* (Taipei: Wenjin, 1996), 333.

2. Qian Qi, "Yu Zhao Ju cha yan," in Anonymous, *Quan Tang shi* (Beijing: Xinhua, 1960), vol. 8, ch. 239, p. 2688.

3. Fu Lingling, "Lu You chashi yanjiu" (master's thesis, Department of Chinese, Qufu Normal University), 17–20.

4. Jiang Yibin, *Song ru yu fojiao* (Taipei: Dongda tushu gongsi, 1997), 43–50.

5. Zhao Ruicai and Zhang Zhonggang, "Zhong wan Tang cha, shi guanxi fawei," *Wenshizhe* 4 (2003): 141.

6. Liao Jianzhi, *Mingdai cha wenhua yishu* (Taipei: Xiuwei, 2007), 176–77, 181–82, 214.

7. Chen Yu and Du Xiaoqin, "Tang Song wenren cha de wenhua yiwen ji qi xingcheng guocheng," *Qinghua Daxue xuebao* 6 (2007): 35–36.

8. Cai Dingyi, "Cong 'chashan' yici guankui Tang Song chashi yu cha wenhua," *Nongye kaogu* 2 (2009): 28–33.

9. Chen and Du, "Tang Song wenren cha de ziran zhi qu," 137; Chen and Du, "Tang Song wenren cha de wenhua yiwen ji qi xingcheng guocheng," 36–38.

10. Lu Yu, *The Classic of Tea*, trans. Francis Ross Carpenter (Hopewell, NJ: Ecco, 1974), 150.

11. Fu, "Lu You chashi yanjiu," 22–25.

12. This trend became particularly pronounced during the Ming dynasty. Liao, *Mingdai cha wenhua yishu*, 180.

13. Shi Shaohua, *Songdai yong chashi yanjiu* (Taipei: Wenjin, 1996), 175–78.

14. James A. Benn, *Tea in China* (Honolulu: University of Hawaii Press, 2015), 36–39, 68–69.

15. Lu, *The Classic of Tea*, 127.

16. Jiao Ran, "Yin cha ge song Zheng Rong," in Anonymous, *Quan Tang shi,* vol. 23, ch. 821, 9262–63.

17. Shi, *Songdai yong chashi yanjiu*, 161–64.

18. Yu Yue and Chen Lingling, "Tang Song chashi zheli zhuiqiu zonglun, *Nongye kaogu* 5 (2010): 156.

19. Lai Gongou, *Cha zhe rui zhi* (Beijing: Guangming ribao, 1999), 28; Li Bincheng, "Tangren yu cha," *Nongye kaogu* 2 (1995): 21.

20. Li, "Tangren yu cha," 22.

21. Jiao Ran, "Gu Zhuxing ji Pei Fangzhou," in Anonymous, *Quan Tang shi,* vol. 23, ch. 821, p. 9266.

22. Song Zian, *Dongxi shi chalu,* in *Zhongguo gudai chayequanshu,* 73.

23. He Mingdong, "Cha yu fojiao," *Nongye kaogu* 2 (1991): 136–37.

24. Liao, *Mingdai cha wenhua yishu*, 184.

25. Ding Yishou, "Jiuhua focha de lishi he yuanyuan," *Chaye tongbao* 27, no. 1 (2005): 43–45.

26. Li Delong, "Dunhuang yishu 'Chajiulun' zhong de chajiu zhengsheng," *Nongye kaogu* 2 (1994): 72.

27. Shen Zuomin, "Fojiao dui Zhongguo chaye fazhan de zuoyong," *Hefei Xueyuan xuebao* 21, no. 2 (2004): 60; He, "Cha yu fojiao," 137.

28. Han Jinke, "Shilun Da Tang cha wenhua," *Nongye kaogu* 2 (1995): 10; Li, "Tangren yu cha," 20–21.

29. Guan Jianping, *Cha yu Zhongguo wenhua* (Beijing: Renmin, 2001), 137–38.

30. James A. Benn, "Buddhism, Alcohol, and Tea in Medieval China," in *Of Tripod and Palate: Food, Politics and Religion in Traditional China*, ed. Roel Sterckx (New York: Palgrave Macmillan, 2005), 221–27.

31. Liu Shufen, "Jielü yu yangsheng zhi jian: Tang Song siyuan zhong de wanyao, ruyao he yaojiu," *Zhongyang Yanjiuyuan Lishi Yuyan Yanjiusuo jikan* 77, no. 3 (2006): 357–99.

32. Jiao Ran, "Jiuri yu Lu Chushi yincha," in Anonymous, *Quan Tang shi,* vol. 23, ch. 817, 9211.

33. Ding Yishou, "Yincha yu chanzong," *Nongye kaogu* 2 (1995): 40; Cao Gonghua, "'Cha chan yi wei' shuo xian yi," *Nongye kaogu* 2 (1991): 145; Nunome Chōhū, *Chūgoku cha no bunkashi* (Tokyo: Kyūbun, 2001), 162–67.

34. Feng Yan, *Fengshi wenjian ji*, in *Qinding siku quanshu* (Taipei: Taiwan shangwu yinshuguan, n.d.), vol. 862, p. 442 (6:1a).

35. Yu and Chen, "Tang Song chashi zheli zhuiqiu zonglun," 154–55.
36. Cao, "'Cha chan yi wei' shuo xian yi," 146.
37. Yu and Chen, "Tang Song chashi zheli zhuiqiu zonglun," 155.
38. Shi, *Songdai yong chashi yanjiu*, 138–44.
39. Lu Yiling, "Cong 'Ru Tang qiufa xunli xingji' kan zhongwan Tang de foshi yinshi," *Dezhou Xueyuan xuebao* 5 (2007): 66–69.
40. Shi, *Songdai yong chashi yanjiu*, 184–89.
41. Zhou Shenghong, "Man ou si ru kan chi wan ying yuan wo shi bie charen," *Mudanjiang Shifan Xueyuan xuebao* 5 (2010): 42.
42. For example in Qian Zhonglian (annot.), *Lu You quanji jiaozhu* (Hangzhou: Zhejiang jiaoyu chubanshe, 2011), vol. 3, p. 453 the poet Lu You describes drinking tea together with a monk amid a wild landscape.
43. Li, "Tangren yu cha," 20.
44. Jiao Ran, "Jiuri yu Lu Chushi yincha," in Anonymous, *Quan Tang shi,* vol. 23, ch. 817, p. 9211.

7

MANHOOD

The meanings and uses of tea steadily amplified during its long evolution from pleasant beverage to profound pursuit. By incorporating aspects of literati culture, Buddhism, Daoism, and many other ideas and practices, tea culture gained sophistication and importance. In particular, the growing diversification of tea culture provided the ambitious drinker with opportunities to display a particular sense of taste and thus craft a unique image for public display, making it a useful tool for the construction of personal identity.

Various kinds of people used tea to distinguish themselves from others and construct a superior social persona. Buddhist monks, emperors, poets, and gentlemen connoisseurs all deployed tea culture somewhat differently. Even so, for all of them the basic goal remained the same. They manipulated tea to stake a claim to some kind of special status, drinking it in ways that could somehow mark them off as better than others. For example, to prove their cultural and social ascendency, literati deliberately complicated tea drinking so that they could then impress onlookers by demonstrating their mastery of its intricacies. The social utility of Chinese tea culture helps account for its sophistication.

Human beings do not interact with each other as unique individuals but via standardized social roles laden with expectations on how different sorts of people ought to behave toward one another. In recognition of this fact, Chinese thinkers did not conceive of the individual in isolation from others, but rather as someone inextricably embedded in the social matrix. According to this way of thinking, the individual cannot be separated from the concomitant roles that create social identity.[1] Moreover, the way a person behaves can vary considerably depending upon the role being enacted at a particular time. A man behaves very differently when performing the role of dutiful son, husband, employer, teacher, or father. Because people perform multiple roles in their lives, they encounter varied opportunities to raise their position in society.

Gender constituted a basic building block of traditional Chinese social relations. In fact, gender can even be considered the most fundamental division in Chinese society. Basic differences between men and women emerged in the Neolithic era, and these distinctions continued to be sharpened and defined as society increased in complexity.[2] Ever since antiquity, writers of various schools have emphasized the importance of distinguishing and separating women from men. Although conventional thinking held that people of both sexes can have achievements, uphold moral values, and live a good life, people assumed that these traits differ considerably for men and women.

Tea culture evolved within a society acutely sensitive to gender difference, with clear distinctions between the roles considered proper for each sex. Given this gendered value system, if a man could somehow use tea to demonstrate a superior form of manhood, he could win respect and raise his standing. This link with masculine identity constitutes one of the most unexpected dimensions of tea's complex history. When men realized that they could deploy tea to demonstrate a superior form of manhood, it became inserted into the innermost dynamics of Chinese social relations.

Although most people think of masculine and feminine as objective biological facts, in fact gendered identity varies considerably. But in spite of this diversity, masculine identity in distant societies nevertheless displays some fundamental features in common. Generally speaking, a man can gain a reputation for proper manhood in two very different ways.[3] In some societies, a young man acquires his masculine identity suddenly by successfully performing a painful or difficult ordeal.[4] If he fails at this rite of passage, he will never be considered a legitimate man. In contrast, whoever succeeds will forever be considered a true man, regardless of his future conduct.

In other places, however, a man builds up a reputation for successful masculinity gradually over the course of a lifetime. By consistently behaving in stereotypically manly ways, he progressively erects a masculine façade that observers around him judge a success. Although men in these cultures avoid an arduous rite of passage, they have to put up with a lifetime of constant stress, as their piecemeal masculine identity remains forever conditional. Just one error or failure, temporarily exposing insufficient manhood, can earn the scorn of popular opinion.

As China lacked a painful adolescent ordeal, it clearly belongs to this second group of cultures. Chinese men calculated their behavior to win the admiration of others and forge a firm masculine identity over the course of a lifetime. But how did they prove themselves authentically masculine? The characteristics making up manhood vary enormously from one society to another. In some places, demonstrating physical strength, pugnacious character, and free spending abandon might be hailed as manly. But during the Tang and Song, elite manhood generally encompassed deliberately refined values. Men constructed a superior masculine identity by demonstrating a familiarity with high culture. The complex culture of tea, which had become ornamented with the trappings of elegance, proved ideal for this purpose.

The connections that developed between tea drinking and heterosexuality also allowed men to display a successful masculine image. Although the elite generally looked down on open displays of carnality, using refined tea culture to express an appreciation for female beauty allowed gentlemen to openly exhibit conventional sexual taste in ways that seemed respectable and even sophisticated. Many Song dynasty poets aroused their readers by evoking scenes of tea being picked, prepared, or served by beautiful women. Some poems describe how courtesans (*geji*) would sing songs in praise of tea before an assembly of male guests.[5] In fact, communal tea drinking during the Song often included entertainment by beautiful women. Patrons might sip tea while listening to them play instruments and sing, or perhaps men would prepare tea after this preliminary entertainment had concluded. Sometimes beautiful women served gentlemen their tea. The women in tea poems always have a much lower social station than the poet, allowing his gaze to dominate her as she carries over his bowl of tea. This sort of tea drinking became a way to confirm a man's claim to superiority on account of his gender.

Despite the attention that poets lavished on beautiful women, the interactions between men mattered far more. Because people act out their social identity when dealing with others, gender often takes on a

The same argument would be made about alcohol

relational meaning. Masculinity constitutes a social performance, with the main target audience consisting of other men rather than women. To judge the success or failure of masculine identity, observers compare men's masculine performances with one another. Many people incorrectly see gender as simply binary—a man is not a woman and vice versa. If this were true, a man could be accepted as truly masculine just by acting differently from women. Yet because women had lower overall status than men and enjoyed far fewer opportunities to publicly socialize with the opposite sex, particularly after the mid-Tang, a man's relation with other men mattered far more to him. Being different and socially superior to women presented no challenge. To construct a successful masculine identity, a man had to interact with other men, gain their acceptance, and convince them to deem his masculine image a success.

Sociologists term these meaningful interactions between men homosociality. During the Tang and Song, elite men regularly gathered together, with each encounter presenting an opportunity for participants to put on a masculine display. Because China's sophisticated tea culture gave men a ready excuse to come together in groups, write poems, read one another's writings, share opinions about connoisseurship, and exchange gifts, tea became an important means for fostering homosocial relations. The conventions of elite tea drinking allowed participants to publicly display the masculine identities they had constructed and hopefully earn approval as proper men.

These cultured groupings became increasingly important as society underwent wrenching transformations. During the late Tang dynasty, the medieval social order grounded in genealogy and hereditary privilege disintegrated.[6] During previous centuries, the greatest families had been those boasting long and prestigious pedigrees. But rising social mobility and an increasingly meritocratic system threw social rankings into confusion. The great families disappeared or lost their monopoly on high office, while minor gentry gained new openings to elevate their station. Some famous families declined into genteel poverty, while talented and ambitious arrivistes climbed the social ladder. The ensuing air of uncertainty made each man eager to somehow prove himself better than his peers. Even men from the best families could no longer simply assume that their status was permanently assured. Stirred by this pervasive sense of insecurity, gentlemen embraced the way of tea, along with other cultured practices, to bind themselves more closely to the elite and claim elevated status. New ways of drinking tea emerged that allowed gentlemen to create and deepen bonds with those of high rank. And when literati came together over the tea table, acceptance into this privileged group allowed each participant to stake a claim to social supremacy.

Tea became a marker of genteel status in numerous ways. For example, by the Tang era, tea had become closely associated with hospitality. Whenever guests arrived, servants automatically boiled a pot of water. Although nowadays serving tea to guests is a standard rule of Chinese etiquette, initially only the most decorous hosts practiced this custom. A cordial gentleman presented guests with a bowl of tea to welcome them and another to see them off.[7] Mastery of these minor social rituals distinguished a man as someone of quality, earning the respect of others who practiced the same conventions.

Tea leaves also made an ideal gift, providing the ambitious gentleman with a way to show off his good taste.[8] Gift giving has played a fundamental role in lubricating Chinese social relations since high antiquity. Because exchanging presents, even items of nominal value, can create or strengthen useful social bonds, this useful custom evolved into a standard ritual. In Confucianism, the exchange of gifts also served to reinforce hierarchy, express aesthetic significance, and socialize those involved.[9] Although people at all levels of society gave gifts to win favor, literati carefully chose items that would convey good taste in order to earn approbation as refined gentlemen. During the Song it became common for literati to confirm their qualifications for membership in this elite group by exchanging small tokens of elegance. Anything associated with writing and art carried considerable cachet: fine paper, writing brushes, ink stones and ink sticks, as well as finished works of calligraphy and painting. Gifts of flowers, fruit, and wine, when chosen correctly, could also display good taste. Tea leaves assumed a respected place among this roster of tasteful gifts.

When men gave and received little gifts of tea, they could deem themselves "tea friends" (*chayou*). Whereas ordinary friendships might be based on a shared enjoyment of base pleasures or a crass desire to network for professional advancement, men who had bonded over tea considered their relationship elevated and pure. Exchanging gifts of tea leaves symbolized not just the depth of their friendship but also shared sentiments and taste, thereby proving that they both belonged to the same exclusive group. Whereas Marxist scholars usually refer to the Song elite simply as landlords, this purely economic definition does not do justice to the manifold aspects of elite identity. To be considered an insider, culture mattered as well. In addition to owning land, a man also had to show proficiency with orthodox academic and cultural pursuits in order to be fully accepted into the literati fraternity. Drinking tea with panache helped prove him worthy of this recognition.

Giving tea to literati friends conveyed a familiarity with what this privileged group regarded as good taste. Of course, when a man sought out a gift that could prove his cultural discrimination, not just any tea would do. Presenting leaves of exceptional quality demonstrated that the giver had the discernment worthy of a true connoisseur. In addition, a local variety, even if not of the highest grade, made a welcome gift to distant tea friends, as this evoked one's locale. A rare or unusual tea also constituted a tasteful gift. And anyone would welcome the arrival of a package containing fine tribute tea, which had not only been rigorously vetted for quality by elaborate bureaucratic procedures but also carried the imprimatur of imperial endorsement. A gentleman might also purchase obscure local teas when traveling and send them to friends as a souvenir that evoked the landscape of a faraway place, using tea as a kind of drinkable postcard.

A literatus usually composed a poem to accompany a gift of tea to a friend. Writing a poem gave him an opportunity to describe the place where the tea originated, the importance of their friendship, a passing emotion experienced while drinking this tea, or a number of other stock themes. In response, the recipient would be obligated to craft another poem, both as a way of thanking the sender for the gift and also to provide a reaction to the contents of the first poem. The resulting back-and-forth turned the exchange of tea and accompanying poetry into an elegant mode of communication among men of letters.

A well-documented custom known as "benevolent tea" (*huicha*) demonstrates the mechanics of giving gifts of tea.[10] During the harvest season, officials stationed in tea producing areas would send gifts of fresh leaves by the fastest possible means to friends residing in distant places. This gift obligated the recipient to send back some local specialty in return, together with a poem of thanks. Some of these poems have been preserved, and they show how men integrated the way of tea together with gift giving and literary culture, using these linked practices to bond themselves together into a cultured elite.

Communal tea drinking presented another major opportunity for homosocial bonding among literati. Brewing, discussing, and enjoying tea together provided a convenient excuse for gentlemen to meet regularly and enjoy cultured pleasures together.[11] Appreciating tea in a deliberately refined manner demonstrated a mastery of the elevated taste that marked one a literatus, allowing the aspiring gentleman to show off his cultural credentials for membership in their closed world. While drinking tea, literati would often participate in other elegant pursuits together as well, such as creating poetry and calligraphy, or discussing the finer points of antiques or gardening. These gentlemanly tea parties became extremely common by the late Tang.

Cultured tea parties gained popularity not just because participants enjoyed tea and convivial company, but also because these frequent gatherings allowed literati to forge a common group identity. Gaining acceptance into a group of tea friends could provide a focal point for a gentleman's social life. Proving one's connoisseurship to these cultivated friends could also win a man acclaim, as they declared experts to be tea men (*charen*) or even tea gods (*chashen*).[12] By closely associating himself with tea, a man could insinuate himself into the heart of literati social life, potentially winning him admiration, prestige, and honor.

Literati realized that tea provided a convenient excuse to meet new contacts, establish friendships, and deepen existing connections. Cultivating true friendship takes time. People can only become close friends if they get together regularly, preferably doing something together that they find interesting and enjoyable. Tea drinking provided a pretext for the repeated meetings necessary to build up close friendships.[13] By providing an excuse for getting together with like-minded people, tea became an important focus for the homosocial networks vital in establishing and maintaining literati identity.

On a more abstract level, tea could also serve as a way to capture and convey memories of past drinking sessions.[14] When a gentleman met his friends frequently over the tea table, he might later, when drinking tea by himself, be reminded of something they had done or said during previous drinking sessions. Tea thus became associated with pleasant memories of past events and activities. Nostalgia evoked by tea drinking inspired poetic competition and also encouraged quiet reflection on the nature of friendship and the cultured life. Sometimes this nostalgia turned into a sort of wistfulness for an idealized past that had never really existed. Because communal tea drinking provided gentlemen with so many memories, it did not merely exist in the present. Tea also shaped their perceptions of the past, giving structure and meaning to memories about friends and their shared cultured pastimes.

Men also frequently wrote poetry together while drinking tea. Today we think of the poet as an isolated figure, laboring in obscurity and virtually ignored. The most influential and cultivated people in imperial China, however, looked on poetry as the supreme art form and made it central to their social life. As poetry writing constituted a central practice of elite homosociality during the rise of tea culture, drinkers inevitably wrote many thousands of poems about tea. Tea poetry did not arise in a vacuum. When men met, they often discussed a wide range of profound issues: politics, social problems, Neo-Confucian philosophy, Buddhism, classical studies, and many other matters. Then they might write poetry together. Because poetry composition took place in such an intellectually rich context, literati positioned their poetry about tea in relation with, and sometimes in reaction to, larger intellectual and political currents, using it to discourse widely about history, politics, ethics, emotions, human character, and the nature of existence.[15] Tea poetry enabled the author to communicate ideas and opinions on a wide range of topics of interest to his peers. Poetry also allowed the writer to show off his erudition. Highly regarded verses often alluded to previous poems, employed archaic diction, referred to historical and mythological figures, and made use of elevated tropes and imagery. Mastering these difficult literary tricks won the poet an enthusiastic response.

The critic Colin Hawes has pointed out that "maintaining friendships was probably the most important function of poetry during this period," explaining that it "acted as a vital channel for initiating and sustaining close relationships with people in positions of power; forming mutually beneficial alliances and support groups with those of one's own social status, or even doing favors to those at lower levels on the social hierarchy."[16] So poetry not only maintained elite circles, but could also break down social barriers. The interactions between monks and literati exemplify the social functions of poetry. By composing poems about a shared love of tea, men from different backgrounds could find common ground based on shared interests and taste, providing them with the basis for good rapport.[17]

Besides exchanging poems about tea and writing poems to accompany gifts of tea, literati often met in groups to drink together and write poems about these genial experiences. Writing poems on a specific topic and critiquing one another's efforts played an important part in literati social life. Gentlemen inserted tea poetry into their salons, making it a standard fixture of refined gatherings. Instead of just allowing each person to write whatever he wanted, literati often played poetry games that allowed everyone in the group to participate in a common literary effort. For example, sometimes when gentlemen gathered together, they would decide to write a series of poems on the same topic using a set rhyme scheme.[18] Or the entire group might write a poem jointly by composing linked verse (*lianju*). Poets dabbled in various types of virtuosic formats and wordplay. By making poetry composition into a kind of communal brainteaser, literati conjured up an atmosphere of elegant fun that strengthened bonds between the members of the group. For example, Lu Yu and his friend Geng Wei wrote a linked verse poem about tea, each of them composing alternate lines to produce a twelve-line poem.[19] While linked verse might not produce the finest literature, playing this sort of sophisticated game brought educated men closer together. And acceptance into a group of male peers allowed each member to partake in the group's overall reputation for successful manhood.

A competitive game based on whipped tea, known as "fighting tea" (*doucha*) or "tea war" (*mingzhan*), provides the most the most dramatic example of how homosociality shaped early tea culture. This amusement grew out of the technique of tea preparation at the time. Tang and Song drinkers whipped tea and hot water together into a frothy infusion in each tea bowl. Stirring the tea rapidly and vigorously with a whisk, described as "skimming tea" (*diancha*), constituted a routine step in the brewing process.[20] Briskly whipping tea dust and hot water together ensured that the beverage infused evenly and quickly. However, this procedure also produced a foamy froth on the surface of the bowl. Connoisseurs not only found this froth attractive, but also claimed that it enhanced the quality of the drink. This archaic whipping technique has been preserved in Japan, where tea masters vigorously beat the tea powder into hot water with a whisk to produce foam that they find desirable, considering the whipping of a proper head of froth an essential step in the tea ceremony. On a far more informal level, a similar appreciation of tea foam also survives in Taiwanese-style bubble tea (*paomo cha*), which is mixed in a cocktail shaker to produce a similar effect.

Tang tea experts considered a thick layer of froth the sign of a well-made bowl of tea. As a result, like battling coffee baristas, tea experts competed with one another to whip up the best *crema*. Because they considered tea making an elegant pursuit, skill at whipping up bubbles became a sign of refinement, and the man with the best froth could enjoy the cries of admiration from his peers. A tea fight basically consisted of each contestant preparing a bowl of tea, taking great pains to perform each step in the process perfectly.[21] First the tea warrior would scrape off the oily protective coating on the compressed disk and gently toast it over a fire, heating it just enough to remove any unwanted flavors that had developed during storage but taking care not to mar the tea with a cooked or burnt taste. Then he cut off a chunk of leaves of the correct size, placed it on a clean sheet of paper, and transferred it to the mortar. He meticulously ground the lump down until the leaves had been reduced to a uniform fine powder. After warming the tea implements to the proper temperature, he scooped the right amount of powder into a bowl, added hot water, and whipped up an impressive head of foam. Throughout this display, the audience expected the contestant to discuss each step in the process, using this monologue to demonstrate both encyclopedic knowledge of tea and also good taste.

Drinkers in Fujian seem to have been the first to stage tea fights.[22] Home to some of the greatest tea, this region pioneered many aspects of tea culture. Archaeologists have even discovered a Song dynasty site on Mount Wuyi in Fujian, a region famed for its tribute teas, that seems to have been a venue for tea fights. Poems describe these contests in detail.[23] From Fujian, competitive tea making spread across China, becoming extremely common among the educated. For example, visitors to famous tea mountains might mark the occasion by staging a tea fight.[24]

Competitive tea soon reached the capital, where it became a common pastime at the imperial court. Emperor Tang Xuanzong engaged in tea fights in his spare time, helping to popularize this game among the elite.[25] And the cultured tea enthusiast Emperor Song Huizong relished tea whipping competitions, presiding over them regularly. Contemporary records describe these events in detail, attesting to their importance in court life.[26] This custom enjoyed such high prestige that it survived even after ground tea had disappeared from the mainstream. During the Ming dynasty, when almost everyone brewed tea in pots using loose leaves, some literati nevertheless kept alive the archaic practice of whipping tea just so they could continue to hold tea fights.[27] They appreciated the difficulty of this technique and also found the bubbles attractive. Most importantly, mastering this antiquated form of tea drinking singled them out as authentic tea connoisseurs.

Besides straightforward competitions to whip up the best head on a bowl of tea, literati invented more complicated tea games as well. Some men enjoyed a game called "divided tea" (*fencha*).[28] After whipping up a generous froth on the top of the tea, contestants would carefully scoop some off with chopsticks or a spoon and use the bubbles to create fanciful shapes, such as animals, birds, insects, fish, and plants. The person judged to have made the best bubble picture won the contest. Another game called "tea command" (*chaling*) developed out of the earlier pastime called wine command (*jiuling*).[29] A person chosen to oversee the game would name an object. Then each participant had to quickly think up a poem or story related to tea that involved the item in question. Those who could not come up with an appropriate anecdote would be fined. This game allowed drinkers to win admiration by showing off their erudition.

Turning tea preparation into a contest made it a way to publicly prove superior manhood. Competition plays an important role in the construction of masculinity. If every man could automatically claim to be suitably masculine, this identity would have no value. Tying manhood to competitive success rendered it important. So even though literati enjoyed cementing their shared elite status through cultured tea parties, they also used these meetings to compete with one another. Introducing an agonistic element into tea culture made it a vehicle for proving successful masculinity.

The increasing complication of tea drinking did not arise by accident. Making tea into such a demanding pursuit, which required participants to memorize a vast body of tea history and literature, raised the level of connoisseurship beyond the capacities of ordinary people, thus allowing tea men to distinguish themselves as members of a male cultural elite. Although people today might dismiss these sorts of games as trivial amusements, Song dynasty gentlemen took tea fights very seriously. A man who gained a reputation as a skillful tea fighter not only gained the respect of his peers, but he might even be invited to serve as an official in tribute tea production, making this pursuit an avenue for professional advancement.[30]

Because tea fights encompassed every aspect of making and appreciating tea, they stimulated the development of connoisseurship, spurring it to new heights. Books describing technical arcana about tea production became numerous and popular largely due to tea fights. Competitors needed to read up on this increasingly complicated subject so that they could impress the judges with their mastery of specialized knowledge. Technical works also set down common standards for assessing skill at tea preparation. To win a tea fight, in addition to whipping up the best foam, participants also had to show off their expertise. A tea warrior might discourse on the nature of particular kinds of leaves, discuss technical aspects of production, and compare the water being used to other sources of fine tea water.

In determining the winner of a tea fight, judges looked mostly at the bubbles floating on the surface.[31] A competitor had to whip the tea until it produced a thick layer of froth that stuck to the sides of the bowl. Generally speaking, the tea fighter whose froth dissipated first, ignominiously exposing the naked liquid underneath, lost the contest. Therefore tea fighters chose water, leaves, and tea ware largely on the basis of what sort of bubbles they would facilitate. This competitive culture forced connoisseurs to ponder what causes tea to yield the most copious froth. Lu You emphasized the importance of good water.[32] He believed that only the right sort of water allowed the tea man to whip up a dense head of foam that would vanquish any competitors. However, other experts, such as Su Shi, stressed the need for high-quality leaves.[33] Su believed that fine tribute tea gave the contestant an indisputable advantage. Cai Xiang considered the creation of durable bubbles a formidable task. He wrote that the proportion of water to powdered leaves has to be optimal, water and tea powder have to be added to the bowl in the right manner, and of course the contestant must whip the mixture properly.[34]

Poets rhapsodized on the beauty of bubbles, taking them to represent the quintessence of tea. Many poems lovingly describe gorgeous bubbles floating on the surface. Their obsession with this trivial detail seems odd until we realize that froth held the key to success in competitive tea.[35] Experts spent considerable time pondering tea foam and debating its ideal characteristics. Some emphasized color, arguing that a pleasant hue distinguishes the best bubbles. Emperor Song Huizong tried to systematize the color of foam by classifying it into four grades. He considered pure white bubbles best, greenish next, grayish third, with yellowish foam the least desirable. However, not everyone considered color paramount. Although the discerning Cai Xiang agreed that bubbles must have the correct tint, whipping up a long-lasting froth that dissipates slowly ultimately wins the tea fight.[36]

Size also mattered. Huizong argued that ideal foam should resemble "millet grain patterns and crab eyes." In other words, the bubbles should be extremely small. Pouring more hot water on the ground leaves to produce successive infusions created different varieties of foam, each consisting of distinctive bubbles. Overall, Huizong believed that the key to good froth does not lie in strength but rather in technique. He revealed the secret to whipping up the best bubbles: proper wrist action.[37]

The aura of painstaking connoisseurship that evolved around competitive tea also led drinkers to select vessels that showed off foam to best advantage. During the Tang, tea drinkers had little interest in dark-colored ceramics. Instead they preferred bowls with a light background that highlighted the color of the liquid, such as simple white Ding ware. But due to the obsessive craze for tea froth that peaked during the Song, colored bowls came into fashion, as a dim background allowed drinkers to see the bubbles most clearly.[38] This shift from lighter-hued vessels toward richly colored wares marked a major shift in the history of Chinese ceramics. Those who preferred fine ceramics sought out exquisitely crafted celadon vessels. But in general, taste swung toward even darker stoneware, such as the black-glazed vessels from Jizhou in what is now Jiangxi province. Potters decorated these bowls with patterns made with paper cuts, or complex glaze effects referred to as tortoiseshell and tiger fur.

The popularity of Jian ware bowls from Fujian during Song, usually known in the West by the Japanese name *tenmoku*, marks a surprising development in Chinese aesthetics. Fujian was home to the finest tribute tea, and drinkers there often served as pioneering tastemakers who

Figure 7.1. Jian ware bowl

moved the way of tea in new directions. After Fujian tea experts began using Jian bowls for their tea fights, drinkers in other regions took notice and began to imitate them. Jian bowls have a distinctive appearance. Instead of striving for smooth even surfaces, craftsmen covered these deliberately simple black vessels with a thick glaze that often runs down the sides, creating thick ripples and drips that seem frozen in time by the firing. This relatively uncontrolled technique creates a simple and almost rustic appearance, an aesthetic diametrically opposite to the exquisitely crafted imperial celadons, whose potters strove for technical perfection.

In embracing Jian ware, literati turned their back on luxurious court taste, preferring to drink their tea from simple dark vessels that harmonized with nature. Not only did the rich black glaze provide a superb background for viewing bubbles, but the steeply sloped sides also suited tea drinking. Unlike rounded bowls, these straight surfaces allowed drinkers to easily slurp down the dregs at the bottom of the bowl. Enthusiasm for Fujian wares stimulated the development of black ceramics in other parts of China, and potters came up with many innovative glazes to satisfy the taste of connoisseurs who demanded dark vessels to best display bubbles during tea fights.[39]

Injecting competition into the way of tea affected far more than just the development of connoisseurship. It also impacted larger aspects of Chinese society and culture. Literati looked to success at tea as a source of prestige that confirmed elite identity. Because success at tea fights won a man acclaim, an elite family might shore up their social standing over the long term by passing down tea lore from father to son. Public competition transformed tea into an undisputed form of cultural capital that families could accumulate, display, and bequeath to their posterity.

Tea men also exchanged leaves among themselves to create bonds and gain prestige. Demand for the most prestigious teas far outstripped supply, and Song literati often complained about their inability to procure the best tea.[40] Poignant longing for the unobtainable became a stock theme of tea poetry. A connoisseur could demonstrate good taste by craving what almost no one could possibly acquire. To solve the problem of acquiring scarce teas, gentlemen gave and received gifts as a way of trading rare leaves among themselves. So if someone obtained a famous tea and served it to friends, he displayed not just good taste but also impressive connections. These social networks binding together important families often persisted for generations. Exchanging rare teas with one another kept these links active and bolstered the collective prestige of everyone in the group.

Men who earned success as tea fighters could teach their offspring how to win competitions, thereby passing down a valuable cultural asset to the next generation. Although books could be extremely helpful, a great deal of tea lore circulated in oral form, constituting a kind of esoteric cultural wisdom that could only be fully transmitted via apprenticeship to a tea master. Someone eager to learn about tea could not simply sign up for formal classes in the subject. He had to find an expert willing to teach him insider tricks and arcana. A father who had accumulated tea expertise would of course pass it on to his sons, giving them a head start in future tea fights that could win honor for themselves and their families.

The integration of tea with other refined activities presented accomplished literati with an ideal opportunity to publicly exhibit their carefully amassed cultural capital. During the Song dynasty, men of letters routinely combined tea drinking with an array of prestigious cultural achievements, such as performing music, playing go, painting and writing, and creating tasteful flower arrangements. Combining tea with other complicated cultural pursuits allowed talented gentlemen to flaunt their cultural achievements, thus staking a claim to high social status in an honor culture that saw cultural accomplishment as a way of demonstrating one's superiority as a man.

Turning tea drinking into a kind of competition took a simple beverage and made it into a way to prove manhood. As in other honor cultures, competition among Chinese men traditionally functioned to form homosocial bonds, demonstrate normative manhood, and establish hierarchy based on success or failure at stereotypical masculine tasks. Even so, competitive events in China tended to be organized somewhat differently from those seen in many other places. The ancient Greeks, for example, usually held contests in open settings visible to the multitude, where men vigorously contended for victory. The Greeks saw competition as a zero-sum game. The entire *polis* lauded the winners, who brought honor not just to themselves but also to their entire community. In contrast, the Chinese elite competed with one another in privileged venues hidden from public view. Maintaining an atmosphere of orderly decorum stood out as their primary objective. Participants cared less about winning than simply joining a prestigious homosocial event while maintaining an air of dignity. Upholding the collective sense of ritual propriety brought honor to all of the participants, even to those who failed to win the tea fight.[41]

Ancient Chinese ideas about the nature and function of competition served as a template for tea fights. Of course a tea man hoped to win the contest. But more importantly, he saw the main point as simply being admitted to the inner circle of tea connoisseurs and carrying out his proper role in the proceedings. The intricacy of tea drinking prior to the rise of the teapot made its preparation an almost ceremonial act. Carrying out this complex social ritual with ease and grace marked someone as a true tea man. If he whipped up the best froth, so much the better. But simply participating in this contest, and performing the ceremony correctly, proved a man's acceptance as an honorable member of the cultural elite. As a result, tea men spent considerable time practicing preparation, studying manuals, memorizing poetry about harvesting tea on misty mountains, and seeking out the right imple-

Figure 7.2. Tea competition

ments. Mastering every aspect of the way of tea provided entrée into a highly prestigious assemblage of cultured gentlemen that certified someone as socially superior.

These numerous links between tea and manhood help explain why Chinese elevated this beverage into such an elaborate pursuit. Men used gifts of tea and shared appreciation during drinking sessions to foster homosociality. These interactions gave them opportunities to evaluate one another's qualifications as honorable men.[42] Although tea might strike outsiders as a trifling pursuit, activities like gift giving and collective drinking sessions played a key role in the construction of masculine identity. Because masculinity takes the form of a social performance, a man needs the right audience. According to the values of this culture, women's opinions of manhood did not carry much weight. Instead, the judgment of other men determined whether someone had succeeded in creating a successful masculine identity. In consequence, members of the elite carefully built up their connections with like-minded gentlemen, engaging in ritualizing gift giving and tea drinking to bring them closer to other men in ways that displayed their cultured masculinity.

By deliberately making tea culture dauntingly complex, literati gained a precious opportunity to prove themselves successful as men. Presenting the right sort of tea (accompanied by a conventional poem) as a gift, or inviting friends over and preparing the drink in the proper manner while making well-informed small talk about tea trivia, marked someone as particularly accomplished, endowing him with the honor associated with orthodox manhood. From today's perspective, forging manhood through tea drinking might seem strangely effete. But to men

Figure 7.3. Whipping Japanese tea

of the Tang and Song, the homosociality of tea drinking provided them with the setting and means for behaving in a consciously cultured manner that people of the time found honorable, thereby proving themselves as superlative men.

Mastery of tea culture also provided gentlemen with valuable social capital. Whereas capital usually refers to material wealth, social capital encompasses the potential value of social ties, which can often be parlayed into tangible benefits.[43] Social capital has numerous important functions. It facilitates the flow of information, thereby allowing people to learn about the relative status, character, and accomplishments of those around them. It also provides the credentials that allow access to key social networks, which in turn provide power and access to resources. Amassing or losing social capital can have an important influence on social identity.

After literati turned tea culture into a common homosocial pursuit among the elite, it became an important source of social capital. Gentlemen used customs such as gift giving, competitive tea drinking, and poetry exchanges as excuses to meet with peers. By drinking tea together, they made new contacts and strengthened existing bonds. For literati, this social capital helped them to maintain their elite social identity. Wealth alone did not define the literatus. He also had to show a facility for cultured pursuits and be accepted as an equal by those in the literati circle. Only if he befriended other literati and they accepted him as one of their own could he truly be considered a member of this elite group. Moreover, in a society where networking and patronage had such an important influence on someone's prospects in life, accumulating social capital could open up opportunities and allow upward mobility.

A group of elite men drinking tea cannot be dismissed as a trivial leisure activity. In fact, gathering together to drink tea had serious consequences for Chinese gentlemen. The drinkers could flaunt their cultural capital and attract new social capital. They cemented their status as literati. And they could use their proficiency in this involved pursuit to construct an honorable masculine identity. All of this and far more could be obtained from a simple bowl of tea.

NOTES

1. Henry Rosemont Jr. and Roger T. Ames, *The Chinese Classic of Family Reverence: A Philosophical Translation of the* Xiaojing (Honolulu: University of Hawaii Press, 2009), 11.

2. Bret Hinsch, "The Origins of Separation of the Sexes in China," *Journal of the American Oriental Society* 123, no. 3 (2003): 595–616.

3. David D. Gilmore, *Manhood in the Making: Cultural Concepts of Masculinity* (New Haven: Yale University Press, 1990), 8, 13.

4. Arnold van Gennep, *The Rites of Passage*, trans. Monika Vizedom and Gabrielle L. Caffee (Chicago: University of Chicago Press, 1960).

5. Yi Shuixia and Hua Chuanguo, "Cong cha shici kan Song dai cha wenhuazhong de nüxing juese," *Nongye kaogu* 2 (2011): 140–41; Shen Songqin, "Liang Song yincha fengsu yu chaci," *Zhejiang Daxue xuebao* 31.1 (2001): 72.

6. Tackett Nicolas, *The Destruction of the Medieval Chinese Aristocracy* (Cambridge, MA: Harvard University Asia Center, 2014); Zhang Bangwei, *Hunyin yu shehui (Songdai)* (Chengdu: Sichuan renmin chubanshe, 1989), 162–63.

7. Shen, "Liang Song yincha fengsu yu chaci," 74–75; Guan Jianping, *Cha yu Zhongguo wenhua* (Beijing: Renmin, 2001), 217–20.

8. Yu Yue and Chen Lingling, "Tang Song chashi zheli zhuiqiu zonglun," *Nongye kaogu* 5 (2010): 161; Shi Shaohua, *Songdai yong chashi yanjiu* (Taipei: Wenjin, 1996), 131; Wen Ye, "Tang Song wenyuan yu chadao wenhua," *Nongye kaogu* 2 (1995): 105; Fu Lingling, "Lu You chashi yanjiu" (master's thesis, Department of Chinese, Qufu Normal University), 7–8.

9. Eric C. Mullis, "Toward a Confucian Ethic of the Gift," *Dao: A Journal of Comparative Philosophy* 7, no. 2 (2008): 175–94.

10. Fang Jian, "Tang Song chali chasu shulue," *Minsu yanjiu* 4 (1998): 77.

11. Yu Yue, *Chalu licheng* (Beijing: Guangming ribao, 1999), 39–40; Shi, *Songdai yong chashi yanjiu*, 113–14.

12. Zhao Ruicai and Zhang Zhonggang, "Zhong wan Tang cha, shi guanxi fawei," *Wenshizhe* 4 (2003): 140–41.

13. Fu, "Lu You chashi yanjiu," 7.

14. Shi, *Songdai yong chashi yanjiu*, 127.

15. Liao Jianzhi, *Mingdai cha wenhua yishu* (Taipei: Xiuwei, 2007), 221.

16. Colin S. C. Hawes, *The Social Circulation of Poetry in the Mid-Northern Song: Emotional Energy and Literati Self-Cultivation* (Albany: State University of New York Press, 2005), 56.

17. Hawes, *The Social Circulation of Poetry in the Mid-Northern Song*, 62.

18. Ibid., 31–50.

19. Wang Guoan and Yao Ying. *Cha yu Zhongguo wenhua* (Shanghai: Hanyu dacidian, 2000), 76–77. For more examples see 77–88.

20. Zhao Tianxiang, "Guanyu 'diancha' 'diantang' zhi yanyi," *Nongye kaogu* 2 (1996): 57. Qiu Jiping, *Songcha tudian* (Hangzhou: Zhejiang sheying, 2004), 32 notes that the term *diancha* often implied more than just whipping tea. It also sometimes referred to appreciating and critically comparing key techniques to determine the winner of a *doucha* competition. Liao Baoxiu, *Songdai chichafa yu chaqi zhi yanjiu* (Taipei: Guoli Gugong Bowuyuan, 1996), 29 explains that *diancha* literally referred to making tea by mixing hot water and ground leaves together in a large bowl. The verb *dian* means pouring hot water into a bowl or cup. Unlike *doucha*, *diancha* did not necessarily stress creating bubbles while whipping up the tea, so it was simpler and more basic than *doucha*. *Diancha* emphasized making good tea, while *doucha* was always competitive.

21. Ke Dongying and Wang Jianrong, "Songdai doucha chutan," *Chaye* 31, no. 2 (2005): 121. For a detailed discussion of criteria used to judge tea fights see Qiu, *Songcha tudian*, 32–63. Also Liao, *Songdai chichafa yu chaqi zhi yanjiu*, 31–35; Ye Yu, *Chajing* (Harbin: Heilongjiang renmin, 2001), 151–57; and Yu, *Chalu licheng*, 101–7.

22. Ke and Wang, "Songdai doucha chutan," 119 and Ye, *Chajing*, 153.

23. Gong Zhi, "Wuyishan faxian Songdai doucha yizhi," *Nongye kaogu* 2 (1994): 114; Lin Gengsheng, "Guanyu 'doucha' de yanjiu," *Nongye kaogu* 4 (1996): 138. For a brief description in English see Victor H. Mair and Erling Hoh, *The True History of Tea* (London: Thames & Hudson, 2009), 62–63.

24. Ye, *Chajing*, 152.

25. Gong Zhi, *Zhongguo gongcha* (Hangzhou: Zhejiang sheying, 2003), 28–29, 34.

26. Lin, "Guanyu 'doucha' de yanjiu," 138–40; Yang Qiusha, "Luetan Songdai doucha yu chaju," *Sichuan wenwu* 4 (1998): 42.

27. Liao, *Mingdai cha wenhua yishu*, 24.

28. For detailed discussions of the origins and evolution of *fencha* see Huang Zhihao, "Song Yuan shidai de fencha yu jiancha," *Nongye kaogu* 5 (2007): 95–99 and Huang Zhihao, "Guanyu Song Yuan shiwenzhong 'fencha' wenti de kaolun," *Zhongguo dianji yu wenhua* 2 (2008): 105–13. Yang Zhishui, "Liang Song chashi yu chashi," *Wenxue yichan* 2 (2003): 69–80 cites many poems that mention *fencha*. Also Fu, "Lu You chashi yanjiu," 6–7.

29. Sun Bipeng, "Tang Song 'doucha,'" *Wenshi zhishi* 3 (1998): 52.

30. Lin, "Guanyu 'doucha' de yanjiu," 138.

31. Zheng Lisheng, "Chamo yu Tangdai cha wenhua," *Nongye kaogu* 2 (1995): 48–49; Ke and Wang, "Songdai doucha chutan," 122.

32. Gu Yunyan, "Lu You de 'Chenyu' yu Songdai de 'doucha,'" *Zhenjiang Gaozhuan xuebao* 2 (2008): 76–78.

33. "Lizhi tan," in Su Shi, *Su Shi quanji* (Shanghai: Shanghai guji, 2000), vol. 1, ch. 39, pp. 483–84.

34. Cai Xiang, *Chalu*, in *Zhongguo gudai chaye quanshu*,65.

35. Sun, "Tang Song 'doucha,'" 51.

36. Cai, *Chalu*, 65–66.

37. Zhao Ji, *Daguan chalun*, in *Zhongguo gudai chaye quanshu*, 92–93.

38. Zhang Liuhe, Yang Runsheng, An Qilin, and Zhang Qing, "Songdai de doucha ji yong zhan," *Shoucangjie* 12 (2009): 70–71.

39. Yang, "Luetan Songdai doucha yu chaju," 43. Tao Zhaojuan and Ruan Qing, "Songren doucha yu Jianyao youzhan," *Chaye* 3 (2008): 190–91. For a survey of the many kinds of dark-toned Chinese ceramics see Robert D. Mowry, *Hare's Fur, Tortoiseshell, and Partridge Feathers: Chinese Brown- and Black-Glazed Ceramics, 400–1400* (Cambridge, MA: Harvard University Art Museums, 1996).

40. Shi, *Songdai yong chashi yanjiu*, 126.

41. Yiqun Zhou, *Festivals, Feasts, and Gender Relations in Ancient China and Greece* (Cambridge: Cambridge University Press, 2010), 98, 157.

42. Eve Kosofsky Sedgwick, *Between Men: English Literature and Male Homosocial Desire* (New York: Columbia University Press, 1985), 1–2; Sharon R. Bird, "Welcome to the Men's Club: Homosociality and the Maintenance of Hegemonic Masculinity," *Gender and Society* 10, no. 2 (1996): 120–32.

43. Nan Lin, *Social Capital: A Theory of Social Structure and Action* (Cambridge: Cambridge University Press, 2001), 20.

GLOSSARY

An Lushan	安祿山
anpin ledao	安貧樂道
Bai Juyi	白居易
Beiyuan	北苑
Bu cha jing	補茶經
buji buli	不即不離
Cai Xiang	蔡襄
cha	茶
cha chan yi wei	茶禪一味
chadao	茶道
Cha jing	茶經
Cha jiu lun	茶酒論
chaliao	茶寮
chaling	茶令
Cha lu	茶錄
chang xin cha cheng sheng yu	嘗新茶呈聖俞
charen	茶人
chashan	茶山
chashen	茶神

Cha shu	茶述
chatang	茶堂
chayan	茶煙
chayou	茶友
Chengtian	承天
chi lengcha	吃冷茶
Chuan fu	荈賦
Daizong	代宗
dao	道
Daodejing	道德經
daoshi	道士
diancha	點茶
Ding (ware)	定
doucha	鬥茶
Du Fu	杜甫
fencha	分茶
fu	賦
gan	甘
geji	歌妓
Geng Wei	耿湋
gewu	格物
gongcha	貢茶
gongshui	貢水
gongxian	貢獻
Guan (ware)	官
guanbei	官焙
Guangshan	光山
Guzhu	顧渚
"Gu Zhuxing ji Pei Fangzhou"	顧渚行寄裴方舟

Huang Ru	黄儒
Huang Tingjian	黄庭堅
huicha	惠茶
Huizong	徽宗
Huoshan	霍山
Huzhou	湖州
Jian (ware)	建
Jian'an	建安
jiande	劍德
Jiangmo	降魔
Jianping	建瓶
jianpu	儉樸
Jianxi	建西
Jiaoran	皎然
Ji Kang	嵇康
Jinling	金陵
Jinsha	金沙
"Jinshi lu houxu"	金石錄後序
Jiuhua (mountain)	九華
jiuling	酒令
"Jiuri yu Lu Chushi yincha"	九日與陸處士飲茶
Jun (ware)	鈞
junzi	君子
kuxin	苦心
"Lanting xu"	蘭亭序
leicha	擂茶
li	禮
lianju	聯句
liao	寮

Li Bai	李白
Li Qingzhao	李清照
lizhi tan	荔支嘆
Longgai	龍蓋
Longjing	龍井
"Lu Tong peng cha tu"	盧仝烹茶圖
Lu You	陸游
Lu Yu	陸羽
maofeng	毛峰
matcha	抹茶
mingong	民貢
mingzhan	茗戰
Naitō Konan	內藤湖南
Nanjing	南京
Ouyang Xiu	歐陽修
paomo cha	泡沫茶
Pei Wen	裴汶
Pincha yaolu	品茶要錄
pu	樸
Qian Qi	錢起
Qian Xuan	錢選
qing (sentiment)	情
qing (purity)	清
Qingming	清明
Qixia	棲霞
qu	曲
Ru (ware)	汝
Ruan Ji	阮籍
Shangcheng	商城

shanseng	山僧
shi	詩
shiseng	詩僧
shixue	視學
Sima Wengong	司馬溫公
Song Huizong	宋徽宗
su	俗
Su Dongpo	蘇東坡
Su Shi	蘇軾
taixue	太學
Taizu	太祖
Tang Taizong	唐太宗
Taoguang	韜光
Tao Qian	陶潛
Tao Yuanming	陶淵明
tenmoku	天目
tian	甜
Tong Hanchen	童漢臣
tu	荼
Wang Xizhi	王羲之
weiqi	圍棋
Wenzong	文宗
xiangshan jushi	香山居士
"Xiao Yi zeng Lanting tu juan"	蕭翼贈蘭亭圖卷
Xiong Fan	熊蕃
Xuanzong	玄宗
ya	雅
Yan Liben	閻立本
Yangzhou	揚州

yi cha yu fan	以茶馭番
Yi jing	易經
"Yin cha ge song Zheng Rong"	飲茶歌送鄭容
yi su wei ya	以俗為雅
Yuan Hongdao	袁宏道
"Yuyuan caicha ge"	御苑採茶歌
"Yu Zhao Ju cha yan"	與趙莒茶讌
Zhiji	智積
zhongyong	中庸
Zhou Feng	周逢
Zhu Xi	朱熹
zisun	紫笋

BIBLIOGRAPHY

Anderson, E. N. *Food and Environment in Early and Medieval China*. Philadelphia: University of Pennsylvania Press, 2014.

———. *The Food of China*. New Haven: Yale University Press, 1988.

Anonymous. *Boxue huishu* 博學彙書. In *Qinding siku quanshu cunmu congshu* 欽定四庫全書存目叢書 (Taipei: Taiwan shangwu yinshuguan, 1995), vol. 3:146 (pp. 590–849) and vol. 3:147 (pp. 1–376).

Anonymous. *Quan Tang shi* 全唐詩. Beijing: Xinhua, 1960.

Anter, Andreas. *Max Weber's Theory of the Modern State: Origins, Structure and Significance*, translated by Keith Tribe. Houndmills, UK: Palgrave Macmillan, 2014.

Benn, James A. "Buddhism, Alcohol, and Tea in Medieval China." In *Of Tripod and Palate: Food, Politics and Religion in Traditional China*, edited by Roel Sterckx. New York: Palgrave Macmillan, 2005, 213–36.

———. *Tea in China: A Religious and Cultural History*. Honolulu: University of Hawaii Press, 2015.

Bird, Sharon R. "Welcome to the Men's Club: Homosociality and the Maintenance of Hegemonic Masculinity." *Gender and Society* 10, no. 2 (1996): 120–32.

Bourdieu, Pierre. *Distinction: A Social Critique of the Judgement of Taste*, translated by Richard Nice. London: Routledge, 1986.

Burckhardt, Jacob. *The Civilization of the Renaissance in Italy*, vol. II, translated by S. G. C. Middlemore. New York: Harper & Row, 1958.

Cai Dingyi 蔡定益. "Cong 'chashan' yici guankui Tang Song chashi yu cha wenhua" 從"茶山"一詞管窺唐宋茶史與茶文化. *Nongye kaogu* 農業考古 2 (2009): 28–33.

Cai Quanbao 蔡泉寶. "Chuan Qin Huzhou zisun lai—Tangdai de gongcha yu gongshui" 傳秦湖州紫笋來－唐代的貢茶與貢水. *Nongye kaogu* 農業考古 2 (1995): 266–67.

Cai Xiang 蔡襄. *Chalu* 茶錄. In *Zhongguo gudai chaye quanshu* 中國古代茶葉全書, edited and annotated by Ruan Haogeng 阮浩耕 et al. Hangzhou: Zhejiang sheying, 1999, 64–70.

Cao Gonghua 曹工化. "'Cha chan yi wei' shuo xian yi" "茶禪一味" 說獻疑. *Nongye kaogu* 農業考古 2 (1991): 145–47.

Castiglione, Baldesar. *The Book of the Courtier*, edited by Daniel Javitch. New York: W.W. Norton & Co., 2002.

Chen Huanliang 陳煥良 and Liang Xiong 梁雄. "'Tu' 'cha' yitong kaolue" "荼" "茶" 異同考略. *Zhongshan Daxue xuebao* 中山大學學報 4 (2002): 77–80.

Chen Qinyu 陳欽育. "Tangdai cha de shengchan yu yunxiao" 唐代茶的生產與運銷. *Gugong wenwu yuekan* 故宮文物月刊 81 (1989): 110–25.

Chen Yu 陳瑜 and Du Xiaoqin 杜曉勤. "Songdai wenren cha de rensheng zhi le" 宋代文人茶的人生之樂. *Wenshi zhishi*文史知識 12 (2007): 91–97.

———. "Tang Song wenren cha de wenhua yiwen ji qi xingcheng guocheng" 唐宋文人茶的文化意蘊及其形成過程. *Qinghua Daxue xuebao* 清華大學學報 6 (2007): 35–44.
Clunas, Craig. *Superfluous Things: Material Culture and Social Status in Early Modern China*. Cambridge: Polity Press, 1991.
Ding Chuan 丁傳. Songren yishi huibian 宋人軼失彙編. Taipei: Taiwan shangwu, 1982.
Ding Yishou 丁以壽. "Jiuhua focha de lishi he yuanyuan" 九華佛茶的歷史和淵源. *Chaye tongbao* 茶葉通報 27, no. 1 (2005): 43–45.
———. "Yincha yu chanzong" 飲茶與禪宗. *Nongye kaogu* 農業考古 2 (1995): 40–41.
Fan Jingduo 樊敬鐸. "Tang Song shidai de chabing" 唐宋時代的茶餅 *Nongye kaogu* 農業考古 4 (1995): 184–86.
Fan Ye 范曄. *Hou Hanshu* 後漢書, annotated by Liu Zhao 劉昭 and Li Xian 李賢 et al. Beijing: Zhonghua shuju, 1965.
Fang Jian 方健. "Tang Song chali chasu shulue" 唐宋茶禮茶俗述略. *Minsu yanjiu* 民俗研究 4 (1998): 74–78.
Fang Yanshou 方彥壽. "Fujian zui zao de tuobenshu – Cai Xiang de 'Chalu'" 福建最早的拓本書 – 蔡襄的 "茶錄." *Yanhuang zongheng* 炎黃縱橫 6 (2007): 51.
Feng Fade 馮法德. "Tianxia mingshan seng zhan bian, conglai senglü duo ai cha – luelun Tangdai Jiao Ran zhuseng chashi" 天下名山僧占遍, 從來僧侶愛茶 – 略論唐代皎然諸僧茶詩. *Nongye kaogu* 農業考古 2 (1995): 192–93.
Feng Yan 封演. *Fengshi wenjian ji* 封氏聞見記. In *Qinding siku quanshu* 欽定四庫全書. Taipei: Taiwan shangwu yinshuguan, n.d., vol. 862, pp. 415–65.
Fingarette, Herbert. *Confucius: The Secular as Sacred*. New York: Harper & Row, 1972.
Fogel, Joshua. *Politics and Sinology: The Case of Naitō Konan, 1866–1934*. Cambridge, MA: Harvard University Asia Center, 1984.
Freeman, Michael. "Sung." In *Food in Chinese Culture: Anthropological and Historical Perspectives*, edited by K. C. Chang. New Haven: Yale University Press, 1977, 146–48.
Fu Lingling 付玲玲. "Lu You chashi yanjiu" 陸游茶詩研究. Master's thesis, Department of Chinese, Qufu Normal University, 2006.
Gilmore, David D. *Manhood in the Making: Cultural Concepts of Masculinity*. New Haven: Yale University Press, 1990.
Gong Zhi 巩志. "Manhua Songdai Beiyuan gongcha" 漫話宋代北苑貢茶. *Nongye kaogu* 農業考古 2 (1998): 209–12.
———. "Wuyishan faxian Songdai doucha yizhi" 武夷山發現宋代斗茶遺址. *Nongye kaogu* 農業考古 2 (1994): 114.
———. *Zhongguo gongcha* 中國貢茶. Hangzhou: Zhejiang sheying, 2003.
Gu Yunyan 顧雲艷. "Lu You de 'Chenyu' yu Songdai de 'doucha'" 陸游的 '晨雨' 與宋代的 '斗茶'. *Zhenjiang Gaozhuan xuebao* 鎮江高專學報 2 (2008): 76–78.
Guan Jianping 關劍平. *Cha yu Zhongguo wenhua* 茶與中國文化. Beijing: Renmin, 2001.
Guo Danying 郭丹英 and Chen Gang 陳鋼. "Song feng zhu lu jiancha—mantan Tangdai chaju" 松風竹爐煎茶—漫談唐代茶具. *Cha bolan* 茶博覽 8 (2009):34–39.
Han Jinke 韓金科. "Shilun Da Tang cha wenhua" 試論大唐茶文化. *Nongye kaogu* 農業考古 2 (1995): 8–14.
Han Shihua 韓世華. "Lun chashi de yuanyuan yu fazhan" 論茶詩的淵源與發展. *Zhongshan Daxue xuebao* 中山大學學報 5 (2000): 59–63.
Hawes, Colin S. C. *The Social Circulation of Poetry in the Mid-Northern Song: Emotional Energy and Literati Self-Cultivation*. Albany: State University of New York Press, 2005.
He Mingdong 何明棟. "Cha yu fojiao" 茶與佛教. *Nongye kaogu* 農業考古 2 (1991): 136–39.
Hinsch, Bret. "The Origins of Separation of the Sexes in China." *Journal of the American Oriental Society* 123, no. 3 (2003): 595–616.
———. "Reconstructing a Lost Chinese Art: Molded Tea Leaves." *Asian-Pacific Culture Quarterly* 26, no. 2 (1998): 63–74.
———. "Textiles and Female Virtue in Early Imperial Chinese Historical Writing." *Nan Nü* 5, no. 2 (2003): 170–202.
Hou Ping 侯萍. "Gudai chafu yanjiu" 古代茶賦研究. *Nongye kaogu* 農業考古 2 (2011): 129–31.

Hu Dan 胡丹. *Chayi fengqing: Zhongguo cha yu shuhua zhuanke yishu de qihe* 茶藝風情: 中國茶與書畫篆刻藝術的契合. Beijing: Guangming ribao, 1999.

Huang Chang 黃裳. *Yinshan ji* 演山集. In *Qinding Siku quanshu* 欽定四庫全書.Taipei: Taiwan shangwu, n.d., vol. 1:1271–86.

Huang, H. T. *Science and Civilization in China*, vol. 6: *Biology and Biological Technology*, part 5, *Fermentations and Food Science*. Cambridge: Cambridge University Press, 2000.

Huang Ru 黃儒. *Pincha yaolu* 品茶要錄. In *Zhongguo gudai chaye quanshu* 中國古代茶葉全書, edited and annotated by Ruan Haogeng 阮浩耕 et al. Hangzhou: Zhejiang sheying, 1999, 77–83.

Huang Yufeng 黃玉鳳. "Wan Tang zhi Song chu fojiao de cha jiu wenhua yanjiu—yi Dunhuang xieben 'Cha jiu lun' wei li" 晚唐至宋初佛教的茶酒文化研究—以敦煌寫本 "茶酒論" 為例. *Wenxuejie* 文學界 8 (2011): 99–101.

Huang Zhihao 黃志浩. "Guanyu Song Yuan shiwenzhong 'fencha' wenti de kaolun" 關於宋元詩文中 "分茶" 問題的考論. *Zhongguo dianji yu wenhua* 中國典籍與文化 2 (2008): 105–13.

———. "Song Yuan shidai de fencha yu jiancha" 宋元時代的分茶與建茶. *Nongye kaogu* 農業考古 5 (2007): 95–99.

Huo Ran 霍然. *Songdai meixue sichao* 宋代美學思潮. Changchun: Changchun chubanshe, 1997.

Jaspers, Karl. *The Origin and Goal of History*, translated by Michael Bullock. London: Routledge, 1953.

Jia Lifang 賈麗芳. "Jianxi Mingchao zhi Zang de junshi sixiang" 簡析明朝治藏的均勢思想. *Xizang Minzu Xueyuan xuebao* 西藏民族學院學報 32, no. 2 (2011): 31–33, 66.

Jiang Yibin 蔣義斌. *Song ru yu fojiao* 宋儒與佛教. Taipei: Dongda tushu gongsi, 1997.

Jin Wenkai 金文凱. "Songdai pincha yishu de shenmei yinsu—cong Su Dongpo de yongcha shi tanqi" 宋代品茗藝術的審美因素—從蘇東坡的咏茶詩談起. *Suihua Xueyuan xuebao* 綏化學院學報 5 (2006): 62–66.

Ke Dongying 柯東英 and Wang Jianrong 王建榮. "Songdai doucha chutan" 宋代鬥茶初探. *Chaye* 茶葉 31, no. 2 (2005): 119–22.

Lai Gongou 賴功歐. *Cha zhe rui zhi: Zhongguo cha wenhua yu ru shi dao* 茶哲睿智: 中國茶文化與儒釋道. Beijing: Guangming ribao, 1999.

Li Bincheng 李斌城. "Tangren yu cha" 唐人與茶. *Nongye kaogu* 農業考古 2 (1995): 15–32.

Li Delong 李德龍. "Dunhuang yishu 'Chajiulun' zhong de chajiu zhengsheng 敦煌遺書 "茶酒論" 中的茶酒爭勝. *Nongye kaogu* 農業考古2 (1994): 72–77.

Li Fei 李飛. "Tang Song chadao daxing zhi yuanyin fenxi" 唐宋茶道大行之原因分析. *Sichuan Ligong Xueyuan xuebao* 四川理工學院學報 25, no. 3 (2010): 61–65.

Li Hui 李暉. "Anhui Tangdai chaye gouchen" 安徽唐代茶葉鉤沈. *Chizhou Xueyuan xuebao* 池州學院學報 23, no. 4 (2009): 87–94.

Li Jing 李菁. "Da yunhe—Tangdai yincha zhi feng de beijian zhi lu" 大運河—唐代飲茶之風的北漸之路. *Zhongguo shehui jingjishi yanjiu* 中國社會經濟史研究 2 (2003): 49–54.

Li Jingde 黎靖德(ed.). *Zhuzi yulei* 朱子語類, annotated by Wang Xingxian 王星賢. Beijing: Zhonghua, 1986.

Li Qian 李芊. "Mantan Song cha de se xiang wei ji qi shenmei fengshang debianhua" 漫談宋茶的色香味及其審美風尚的變化. *Nongye kaogu* 農業考古4 (2011): 79–83.

Li Qingzhao 李清照. *Li Qingzhao ji jianzhu* 李清照集箋注, annotated by Xu Peijun 徐培均. Shanghai: Shanghai guji, 2002.

Liang Zi 梁子. "Bai Juyi guju chutu chaqi" 白居易故居出土茶器. *Nongye kaogu* 農業考古 4 (1995): 84.

Liao Baoxiu 廖寶秀. *Songdai chichafa yu chaqi zhi yanjiu* 宋代喫茶法與茶器之研究. Taipei: Guoli Gugong Bowuyuan, 1996.

Liao Jianzhi 廖建智. *Mingdai cha wenhua yishu* 明代茶文化藝術. Taipei: Xiuwei, 2007.

Lin Anjun 林安君. "Cong Yan Liben 'Xiao Yi zeng Lanting tujuan' tan Tangdai cha wenhua" 從閻立本 '蕭翼贈蘭亭圖卷' 談唐代茶文化. *Nongye kaogu* 農業考古 2 (1995): 221–23.

Lin Gengsheng 林更生. "Guanyu 'doucha' de yanjiu" 關於 "斗茶" 的研究. *Nongyekaogu* 農業考古 4 (1996): 138–40.

Lin Jiali 林家驪 and Yang Jian 楊健. "Tang Wudai chashi de fazhan yanbian ji qiwenhua fengmao" 唐五代茶詩的發展演變及其文化風貌. *Zhejiang Shuren Daxue xuebao* 浙江樹人大學學報 11, no. 4 (2011): 52–57.

Lin, Nan. *Social Capital: A Theory of Social Structure and Action*. Cambridge: Cambridge University Press, 2001.

Liu Jing 劉靜. "Tangren yong Lu Yu shi yanjiu: cha he Lu Yu de shenghuo, 'Cha jing' de xiezuo ji qi rensheng chutan" 唐人咏陸羽詩研究茶和陸羽的生活茶經的寫作及其人生初探. *Nongye kaogu* 農業考古 2 (2011): 132–38.

Liu Shufen 劉淑芬. "Jielü yu yangsheng zhi jian—Tang Song siyuan zhong de wanyao, ruyao he yaojiu" 戒律與養生之間—唐宋寺院中的丸藥乳藥和藥酒. *Zhongyang Yanjiuyuan Lishi Yuyan Yanjiusuo jikan* 中央研究院歷史語言研究所集刊 77, no. 3 (2006): 357–99.

Liu Wenzhi 劉蘊之. "'Shuipin' bianzheng" "水品" 辨証. *Guji zhengli yanjiu xuekan*古籍整理研究學刊 6 (1995): 35–37.

Liu Xuezhong 劉學忠. "Cong jiu dao cha—gudai wenren de renge yanbian zongtan" 從酒到茶—古代文人的人格演變縱探. *Fuyang Shiyuan xuebao* 阜陽師院學報 4 (1995): 28–33, 53.

———. "Zhongguo gudai chaguan kaolun" 中國古代茶館考論. *Shehui kexue zhanxian* 社會科學戰線 5 (1994): 120–25.

Lu Jianwei 陸建偉. "Lu Yu sixiangzhong de chanxing yixiang" 陸羽思想中的禪性意向. *Huzhou Shizhuan xuebao* 湖州師專學報 2 (1996): 52–55.

Lü Weixin 呂維新. "Tangdai gongcha zhidu de xingcheng he fazhan" 唐代貢茶制度的形成和發展. *Chaye tongbao* 茶葉通報 1 (1995): 257–59.

Lu Yiling 陸宜玲. "Cong 'Ru Tang qiufa xunli xingji' kan zhongwan Tang de foshi yinshi" 從"入唐求法巡禮行紀" 看中晚唐的佛事飲食. *Dezhou Xueyuan xuebao* 德州學院學報 5 (2007): 66–69.

Lu Yu 陸羽. *Cha jing jiaozhu* 茶經校注, annotated by Shen Dongmei 沈冬梅. Taipei: Yuhe Wenhua, 2009.

Lu Yü. *The Classic of Tea: Origins & Rituals,* translated by Francis Ross Carpenter. Hopewell, NJ: Ecco, 1974.

Mair, Victor H., and Erling Hoh. *The True History of Tea*. London: Thames & Hudson, 2009.

Mao Wenxi 毛文錫. *Chapu* 茶譜. In *Zhongguo gudai chaye quanshu* 中國古代茶葉全書, edited and annotated by Ruan Haogeng 阮浩耕 et al. Hangzhou: Zhejiang sheying, 1999, 45–49.

Mauss, Marcel. *The Gift: The Form and Reason for Exchange in Archaic Societies*, translated by W. D. Halls. New York: W.W. Norton & Co., 2000.

Mowry, Robert D. *Hare's Fur, Tortoiseshell, and Partridge Feathers: Chinese Brown- and Black-Glazed Ceramics, 400–1400*. Cambridge, MA: Harvard University Art Museums, 1996.

Mullis, Eric C. "Toward a Confucian Ethic of the Gift." *Dao: A Journal of Comparative Philosophy* 7, no. 2 (2008): 175–94.

Nunome Chōhū 布目潮渢. *Chūgoku cha no bunkashi* 中國茶の文化史. Tokyo: Kyūbun, 2001.

Ouyang Xiu 歐陽修. *Ouyang Xiu quanji* 歐陽修全集. Beijing: Zhonghua, 2001.

Pei Wen 裴汶. *Chashu* 茶述. In *Zhongguo gudai chaye quanshu* 中國古代茶葉全書, edited and annotated by Ruan Haogeng 阮浩耕 et al. Hangzhou: Zhejiang sheying, 1999, 26–67.

Qian Zhonglian 錢仲聯 (annot.). *Lu You quanji jiaozhu* 陸游全集校注. Hangzhou: Zhejiang jiaoyu chubanshe, 2011 (13 vols.).

Qiu Jiping 裘紀平. *Songcha tudian* 宋茶圖典. Hangzhou: Zhejiang sheying, 2004.

Rosemont, Henry Jr., and Roger T. Ames. *The Chinese Classic of Family Reverence: A Philosophical Translation of the* Xiaojing. Honolulu: University of Hawaii Press, 2009.

Ruggiero, Guido. *The Renaissance in Italy: A Social and Cultural History of the Rinascimento.* Cambridge: Cambridge University Press, 2014.

Schwartz, Benjamin I. *The World of Thought in Ancient China*. Cambridge, MA: The Belknap Press of Harvard University Press, 1985.

Sedgwick, Eve Kosofsky. *Between Men: English Literature and Male Homosocial Desire*. New York: Columbia University Press, 1985.

Shen Dongmei 沈冬梅. "Lun Songdai Beiyuan guanbei gongcha" 論宋代北苑官焙貢茶. *Zhejiang shehui kexue* 浙江社會科學 7 (1997): 98–102.

Shen Gua 沈括. *Benchao chafa* 本朝茶法. In *Zhongguo gudai chaye quanshu* 中國古代茶葉全書, edited and annotated by Ruan Haogeng 阮浩耕 et al. Hangzhou: Zhejiang sheying, 1999, 84–88.

Shen Songqin 沈松勤. "Liang Song yincha fengsu yu chaci" 兩宋飲茶風俗與茶詞. *Zhejiang Daxue xuebao* 浙江大學學報 31, no. 1 (2001): 70–76.

Shen Zuomin 沈佐民. "Fojiao dui Zhongguo chaye fazhan de zuoyong" 佛教對中國茶葉發展的作用. *Hefei Xueyuan xuebao* 合肥學院學報 21, no. 2 (2004): 59–62.

Shi Shaohua 石韶華. *Songdai yong chashi yanjiu* 宋代詠茶詩研究. Taipei: Wenjin, 1996.

Shu Yujie 舒玉杰. *Zhongguo cha wenhua jingo daguan* 中國茶文化今古大觀. Beijing: Dianzi gongye, 1999.

Song Houling 宋后玲. "Chahua, chahua" 茶話, 茶畫. *Gugong wenwu yuekan* 故宮文物月刊 4 (1983): 103–7.

Song Zian 宋子安. *Dongxi shi chalu* 東溪試茶錄. In *Zhongguo gudai chayequanshu* 中國古代茶葉全書. Edited and annotated by Ruan Haogeng 阮浩耕 et al. Hangzhou: Zhejiang sheying, 1999, 71–76.

Su Shi 蘇軾. *Su Shi quanji* 蘇軾全集. Shanghai: Shanghai guji, 2000.

Sun Bipeng 孫必鵬. "Tang Song 'doucha'" 唐宋 "斗茶." *Wenshi zhishi* 文史知識 3(1998): 50–52.

Sun Hongsheng 孫洪升. *Tang Song chaye jingji* 唐宋茶業經濟. Beijing: Shehui kexue wenxian, 2001.

Tackett, Nicolas. *The Destruction of the Medieval Chinese Aristocracy*. Cambridge, MA: Harvard University Asia Center, 2014.

Tao Zhaojuan 陶兆娟 and Ruan Qing 阮倩. "Songren doucha yu Jianyao youzhan" 宋人斗茶與建窯釉盞. *Chaye* 茶葉 3 (2008): 190–91.

Tong Qiqing 童啓慶. "Tang Song shiqi Zhejiang cha wenhua de fazhan" 唐宋時期浙江茶文化的發展. *Nongye kaogu* 農業考古 4 (1997): 26–32, 37.

van Gennep, Arnold. *The Rites of Passage*, translated by Monika Vizedom and Gabrielle L. Caffee. Chicago: University of Chicago Press, 1960.

Wang Cangxi 王倉西 and Tian Shenghua 田生華. "Famensi ta digong chutu chaju yu 'Cha jing—si zhi qi' duibi yanjiu" 法門寺塔地宮出土茶具與 "茶經—四之器" 對比研究. *Nongye kaogu* 農業考古 2 (1995): 168–71.

Wang Fu 王敷. *Cha jiu lun* 茶酒論. In *Zhongguo gudai chaye quanshu* 中國古代茶葉全書, edited and annotated by Ruan Haogeng 阮浩耕 et al. Hangzhou: Zhejiang sheying, 1999, 39–44.

Wang Guoan 王國安 and Yao Ying 要英. *Cha yu Zhongguo wenhua* 茶與中國文化. Shanghai: Hanyu dacidian, 2000.

Wang He 王河. "Tang Song gu yi chashu gouchen" 唐宋古逸茶書鈎沈. *Nongye kaogu* 農業考古 2 (1998): 263–68.

Wang Jianping 王建平. *Chaju qingya: Zhongguo chaju yishu yu jianshang* 茶具清雅: 中國茶具藝術與鑒賞. Beijing: Guangming ribao, 1999.

Wang Lin 王林 and Zhang Wei 張威. "Tang zisun gongcha yanjiu" 唐紫笋貢茶研究. *Anhui wenxue* 安徽文學 9 (2010): 143–44.

Wang Shuanghuai 王雙懷. "Lun Tangdai yincha fengqi xingcheng de yuanyin" 論唐代飲茶風氣形成的原因. *Nongye kaogu* 農業考古 4 (1998): 41–45.

Wang Xinxing 王欣星. "Cha yu Songren shang 'qing' de meixueguan" 茶與宋人尚 "清" 的美學觀. *Jingchu Ligong Xueyuan xuebao* 荊楚理工學院學報 25, no.10 (2010): 46–48.

Wang Xinying 王馨英. Tangdai tugong zhidu tanxi 唐代土貢制度探析. *Tianzhong xuekan* 天中學刊 27, no. 5 (2012): 90–93.

Wang Yongping 王永平. "Tangdai gongting yincha" 唐代宮廷飲茶. *Yinshi wenhua yanjiu* 飲食文化研究 13, no. 1 (2005): 98–102.

Wen Tingyun 溫庭筠. *Caicha lu* 采茶錄. In *Zhongguo gudai chaye quanshu* 中國古代茶葉全書, edited and annotated by Ruan Haogeng 阮浩耕 et al. Hangzhou: Zhejiang sheying, 1999, 37–38.

Wen Ye 文野. "Tang Song wenyuan yu chadao wenhua" 唐宋文苑與茶道文化. *Nongye kaogu* 農業考古 2 (1995): 103–6.

Wilson, Thomas M. "Drinking Cultures: Sites and Practices in the Production and Expression of Identity." In *Drinking Cultures*, edited by Thomas M. Wilson. Oxford: Berg, 2005, 1–24.

Wu Shuijin 吳水金 and Chen Weiming 陳偉明. "Song shi yu cha wenhua" 宋詩與茶文化. *Nongye kaogu* 農業考古 4 (2001): 173–75.

Wu Siqiang 吳思強. "Su Dongpo de zhucha jing" 蘇東坡的煮茶經. *Cha bolan* 茶博覽 11 (2010): 60–61.

Wu Zimu 吳自牧. *Mengliang lu* 夢梁錄. Taipei: Zhonghua, 1985.

Xie Baocheng 謝保成, "Xie 'Li Bai yu Du Fu' de 'kuxin' guyi" 寫 "李白與杜甫" 的 "苦心" 孤詣, *Guo Moruo xuekan* 郭沫若學刊 2 (2012): 60–63.

Xiong Fan 熊蕃. *Xuanhe Beiyuan gongcha lu* 宣和北苑貢茶錄. In *Qinding siku quanshu* 欽定四庫全書. Taipei: Taiwan shangwu yinshuguan, n.d., vol. 844, pp. 637–47.

Xu Jingmei 徐京美. "Songdai chashizhong de gongcha caizhi tese" 宋代茶詩中的貢茶采制特色. *Dazhong wenyi* 大眾文藝 12 (2011): 167–68.

Xue Qiao 薛翹 and Liu Jinfeng 劉勁峰. "Woguo Han Tang cha wenhua de huohuashi—leicha" 我國漢唐茶文化的活化石—擂茶. *Nongye kaogu* 農業考古 2 (1995): 143–46.

Yang Qiusha 楊秋莎. "Luetan Songdai doucha yu chaju" 略談宋代斗茶與茶具. *Sichuan wenwu* 四川文物 4 (1998): 42–44.

Yang Quhui 楊旭輝. "Xikunti de xingcheng ji qi dui Songdai shifeng de kaichuang yiyi" 西昆體的形成及其對宋代詩風的開創意義. *Changshou gaozhuanxuebao* 常熟高專學報 1 (1995): 27–30, 85.

Yang Xun 楊洵. "Jian yao tuhao zhan de xingqi yu Songdai gongting douche wenhua" 建窯兔毫盞的興起與宋代宮廷斗茶文化. Shoudu Shifan Daxue xuebao 首都師範大學學報 (2011): 72–74.

Yang Zhishui 揚之水. "Liang Song chashi yu chashi" 兩宋茶詩與茶事. *Wenxueyichan* 文學遺產 2 (2003): 69–80.

Yang Zihua 楊子華. "'Shuihu' yu Song Yuan Hangzhou de cha wenhua" "水滸" 與宋元杭州的茶文化. *Yuanyang Shifan Gaodeng Zhuanke Xuexiao xuebao* 隕陽師範高等專科學校學報 28, no. 2 (2008): 29–33.

Ye Yu 葉羽. *Chajing* 茶經. Harbin: Heilongjiang renmin, 2001.

Yi Shuixia 易水霞 and Hua Chuanguo 花傳國. "Cong cha shici kan Song dai cha wenhuazhong de nüxing juese" 從茶詩詞看宋代茶文化中的女性角色. *Nongye kaogu* 農業考古 2 (2011): 139–43.

Yu Wenxia 虞文霞. "Cong 'Daguan chalun' kan Song Huizong de cha wenhua qingjie ji Songren chadao" 從 "大觀茶論" 看宋徽宗的茶文化情結及宋人茶道. *Nongye kaogu* 農業考古 2 (2005): 60–64.

Yu Yue 余悅. *Chalu licheng: Zhongguo cha wenhua liubian jianshi* 茶路歷程: 中國茶文化流變簡史. Beijing: Guangming ribao, 1999.

Yu Yue 余悅 and Chen Lingling 陳玲玲. "Tang Song chashi zheli zhuiqiu zonglun" 唐宋茶詩哲理追求綜論. *Nongye kaogu* 農業考古 5 (2010): 154–70.

Yuan Jixi 袁濟喜. *Renhai guzhou – Han Wei liuchao shi de gudu yishi* 人海孤舟－ 漢魏六朝士的孤獨意識. Zhengzhou: Henan renmin, 1995.

Zhang Bangwei 張邦煒. *Hunyin yu shehui (Songdai)* 婚姻與社會 (宋代). Chengdu: Sichuan renmin chubanshe, 1989.

Zhang Liuhe 張柳河, Yang Runsheng 楊潤生, An Qilin 安奇林 and Zhang Qing 張倩. "Songdai de doucha ji yong zhan" 宋代的斗茶及用盞. *Shoucangjie* 收藏界 12 (2009): 70–71.

Zhang Youxin 張又新. *Jiancha shuiji* 煎茶水記. In *Zhongguo gudai chaye quanshu* 中國古代茶葉全書, edited and annotated by Ruan Haogeng 阮浩耕 et al. Hangzhou: Zhejiang sheying, 1999, 28–30.

Zhang Zexian 張澤咸. "Han Tang shiqi de chaye" 漢唐時期的茶葉. *Wenshi* 文史 11 (1981): 61–79.
Zhao Hengfu 趙恆富. "Tang Song chazhan yu yincha yishu" 唐宋茶盞與飲茶藝術. *Wenwu shijie* 文物世界 6 (2001): 49–51.
Zhao Hongju 趙紅菊. "Luelun Wei Jin yongwu shi de guoduxing yiyi" 略論魏晉詠物詩的過渡性意義. *Nei Menggu Daxue xuebao* 內蒙古大學學報 45, no. 1 (2013): 98–101.
Zhao Hui 趙輝. *Liuchao shehui wenhua xintai* 六朝社會文化心態. Taipei: Wenjin, 1996.
Zhao Ji 趙佶. *Daguan chalun* 大觀茶論. In *Zhongguo gudai chaye quanshu* 中國古代茶葉全書, edited and annotated by Ruan Haogeng阮浩耕 et al. Hangzhou: Zhejiang sheying, 1999.
Zhao Ruicai 趙睿才 and Zhang Zhonggang 張忠剛. "Zhong wan Tang cha, shi guanxi fawei" 中晚唐茶, 詩關係發微. *Wenshizhe* 文史哲 4 (2003): 140–44.
Zhao Tianxiang 趙天相. "Guanyu 'diancha' 'diantang' zhi yanyi" 關於 "點茶" "點湯"之衍義. *Nongye kaogu* 農業考古 2 (1996): 57–58.
Zheng Lisheng 鄭立盛. "Beiyuan chashi" 北苑茶史. *Nongye kaogu* 農業考古 2 (1991): 203–7.
———. "Chamo yu Tangdai cha wenhua" 茶沫與唐代茶文. *Nongye kaogu* 農業考古 2 (1995): 48–49.
Zhou Feng 周逢. *Bu cha jing* 補茶經. In *Zhongguo gudai chaye quanshu* 中國古代茶葉全書, edited and annotated by Ruan Haogeng 阮浩耕 et al. Hangzhou: Zhejiang sheying, 1999, 57–58.
Zhou Hui 周慧. "Chali xingcheng yuanyin shulun" 茶禮形成原因述論. *Shenyang Hangkong Gongye Xueyuan xuebao* 瀋陽航空工業學院學報 23, no. 6 (2006): 88–90.
Zhou Mi 周密. *Wulin jiushi* 武林舊事. In *Jingyin Wenyuange Siku quanshu* 景印文淵閣四庫, edited by Ji Yun 紀昀 et al. Taipei: Taiwan shangwu, 1983, v. 590, pp. 173–299.
Zhou Shenghong 周聖弘. "Man ou si ru kan chi wan ying yuan wo shi bie charen: Bai Juyi chashi shuping" 滿甌似乳堪持玩應緣我是別茶人: 白居易茶詩述評. *Mudanjiang Shifan Xueyuan xuebao* 牡丹江師範學院學報 5 (2010): 40–45.
Zhou, Yiqun. *Festivals, Feasts, and Gender Relations in Ancient China and Greece*. Cambridge: Cambridge University Press, 2010.
Zhu Nailiang 朱乃良. "Tangdai cha wenhua yu Lu Yu 'Cha jing'" 唐代茶文化與陸羽 "茶經." *Nongye kaogu* 農業考古 2 (1995): 58–62.
Zhu Zhongsheng 朱重聖. *Bei Song cha zhi shengchan yu jingji* 北宋茶之生產與經濟. Taipei: Taiwan xuesheng, 1985.
Zhu Zizhen 朱自振. *Chashi chutan*茶史初探. Beijing: Zhongguo nongye, 1996.
———. "Guanyu 'cha' zi chuyu zhong Tang de kuangzheng" 關於"茶" 字出於中唐的匡正. *Gujin nongye* 古今農業 2 (1996): 42–46.

INDEX

ABOUT THE AUTHOR

Bret Hinsch is professor in the Department of History at Fo Guang University, Yilan, Taiwan. He is the author of *Masculinities in Chinese History*, *Women in Early Imperial China*, and *Passions of the Cut Sleeve: The Male Homosexual Tradition in China.*